SONGS *of* PRAISE
for
BOYS & GIRLS

Songs of Praise
for
Boys and Girls

By

Percy Dearmer

R. Vaughan Williams

Martin Shaw

Oxford University Press
London: Humphrey Milford
1929

OXFORD UNIVERSITY PRESS
AMEN HOUSE, E.C. 4
LONDON EDINBURGH GLASGOW
LEIPZIG NEW YORK TORONTO
MELBOURNE CAPETOWN BOMBAY
CALCUTTA MADRAS SHANGHAI
HUMPHREY MILFORD
PUBLISHER TO THE
UNIVERSITY

Printed in Great Britain

PREFACE

THIS book is for young people of all ages, including even the very young, for whom there are some little songs which they can easily learn by heart. Although age cannot be measured by years, it may be stated broadly that this book is intended on the whole for those between the ages of seven and seventeen. The numbers specially suitable also for those still younger are marked with the sign °; and to these must be added the short Kindergarten hymns which are printed among *Short Services*. But no such attempt at grading can be final: some quite young children will show a remarkable understanding of adult hymns (e.g. Nos. 24 and 37)—and a word not understood often has great 'semantic' value for young and old alike; on the other hand, some children's hymns like 'All things bright and beautiful' are now among the most popular of adult hymns, especially when sung to the delightful tune in *Songs of Praise* (here printed as No. 38), and one at least of our new children's hymns, 'Glad that I live am I' (No. 49), has already been seized upon with conviction by many a burly adult. Indeed in many cases what makes children's hymns unsuitable for the grown-ups is that they are not really childlike (as Blake, for instance, is childlike): there is a mass of hymns written for the young by excellent didactic persons, who often betray themselves by harping on the word 'little'—till it becomes almost an expletive, and who put into the mouth of the unsuspecting adolescent words which express, not what the child is, but what they fancy a child ought to be. When the priggish and unwholesome elements are excluded, the number of real children's hymns is small enough. After all, the application of psychology to the various ages of man is of recent introduction; and in the ages when boys and girls came creeping like snails to the fount of knowledge, many of the hymns provided for them may be described as dwarf hymns, rather than hymns for children. The field of selection is therefore really a small one. Nevertheless some old writers found the way by intuition; and therefore there are a few classics, and others of lesser rank which hold a well-deserved place in our affections.

We have included also some of the best of the normal hymns for adults: hymns like the Old Hundredth are sufficiently direct in thought for most boys and girls within our category, and they

PREFACE

help to form a link with maturer years. None of them, we estimate, are unsuitable in words or music for fairly educated young people of ten years or thereabouts, though it is good to practise a new tune, and sometimes to explain a phrase. Indeed an important feature of some hymns seems to be the opportunity which they give of drawing out the meaning of a word, such as the 'wind' as an illustration of the reality and power of unseen things, or 'disputes' as implying the League of Nations and the hope of continued improvement in the industrial and social order. Moreover, occasions arise when it is extremely convenient to have at hand a few hymns that are suitable also for adults.

With some editions of *Songs of Praise for Boys and Girls* is included a collection of *Short Services*, which it is hoped may serve as a convenient manual for those who conduct free services for adults, as well as for those who are concerned mainly with children. This collection places the more suitable short Psalms and the Canticles, with a few simple prayers and litanies, at the disposal of the minister.

NOTE

The sign ° means that the hymn is specially suitable for little children, though not necessarily unsuitable for adults also. Many of the other hymns are also suitable for the very young, with a little practice and explanation. The sign * means that a verse may be omitted without detriment to the sense; † that an alteration has been made in one line of the original, and ‡ that alterations have been made in two or three lines. In the case of No. 2, more had to be changed in order to fit the poem for singing: no. 9, in the form taken down from an old woman in Tavistock, had four verses, which are accessible in *English Folk-Songs for Schools* (Curwen) and in *Song Time* (Curwen), and contains a few obvious corruptions of the lost original. *Tr.* means 'translated by'; *Ps.* means 'Psalm'. The verses are numbered, and a full point after a number indicates the last verse. It is suggested that 'Amen' should at most only be sung after the Doxologies.

ACKNOWLEDGEMENTS

Thanks are due to the following Authors, Composers, and Copyright owners for permission to include their Hymns and Tunes, viz.:

Hymns: Mr. H. N. Brailsford, 39; Mrs. Canton, 5, 91; Mrs. Chesterton, 58; Rev. Canon J. M. C. Crum, 81; Messrs. J. Curwen & Sons, 61 (from Curwen Edition No. 5454); English Hymnal Committee, 23, 56; Trustees of the Fellowship Hymn Book, 87; Mr. F. D. How, 64; Mrs. E. Rutter Leatham, 103; Messrs. Macmillan & Co., 92; Rev. Walter J. Mathams, 66; Estate of the late Mr. Thomas B. Mosher, 49; National Society, 89; National Sunday School Union, 52, 55, 60; Oxford University Press, 3, 12, 53, 59, 97; Messrs. A. W. Ridley & Co., 9, 10; Mr. R. C. Trevelyan, 19; Mr. Steuart Wilson, 62, 90.

The Editors also acknowledge the copyright hymns under the initials M. D., N. B. L., P. D., and S. P.; also Nos. 40, 73, 77, and 111.

Tunes: Miss Nora M. Bicknell, 27; Messrs. J. Curwen & Sons, 31, 48, 67 (from Curwen Edition No. 6300), 38 (from Curwen Edition No. 80629), 51 (from Curwen Edition No. 71655), 88, 98, 102 (from Curwen Edition No. 8606), 99 (from Curwen Edition No. 80667), 106 (from Curwen Edition No. 80644); Mr. K. G. Finlay, 52; Miss Imogen Holst, 79^1; Hope Publishing Company, Chicago, 82; Miss Maud Karpeles (for melodies of Nos. 29^1, 29^2, 58, 72, 77, 78, 89); Ven. Archdeacon Kewley, 90 (melody); Mr. R. O. Morris, 50^1; Messrs. A. R. Mowbray & Co., 17; National Sunday School Union, 55; Messrs. A. W. Ridley & Co., 9 (melody), 10; Professor Julius Röntgen, 19; Mr. Geoffrey Shaw, 85, 96; Messrs. N. Simrock, and Alfred Lengnick & Co. Ltd., 111; Sir Arthur Somervell, 45; Dr. J. Lloyd Williams, 42 (melody); Rev. Canon David F. R. Wilson, 61.

The following tunes and harmonizations are the copyright of the Musical Editors: 1, 9, 13, 18, 20, 22, 23, 27, 29^1, 29^2, 33, 39, 40, 41, 42, 47, 56, 57, 58, 60, 62, 64, 65, 72, 77, 78, 80, 81, 83, 84, 86, 89, 90, 93, 94, 95, 103, 105, 109^1, 109^2.

The following tunes and harmonizations are the copyright of the Oxford University Press: 2, 3, 5, 8, 12, 15, 43, 46, 49, 50^2, 53, 54, 66, 69, 76, 79^2, 87, 91, 92, 107, 108^1, 108^2, 108^3.

The Editors also thank the following, who have composed tunes especially for this book: Rev. Canon G. W. Briggs, Miss Evelyn Sharpe, Mr. Geoffrey Shaw, Mr. Gordon Slater.

CONTENTS

PART I. TIMES AND SEASONS

PART II. GENERAL HYMNS

PART III. SPECIAL HYMNS

PART I
TIMES AND SEASONS

Morning and Evening
Spring to Winter
Christmas to Whitsuntide
Angels and Saints

1   HARDWICK.   (6 5. 6 5.   Irregular.)

In moderate time.   Unison.   English Traditional Melody.

(Copyright, 1925, by R. Vaughan Williams.)

Time.   *Thomas Carlyle, 1795–1881.*

SO here hath been dawning
    Another blue day:
Think, wilt thou let it
    Slip useless away?

2 Out of eternity
    This new day is born;
Into eternity,
    At night, will return.

3 Behold it aforetime
    No eye ever did:
So soon it forever
    From all eyes is hid.

4. Here hath been dawning
    Another blue day:
Think, wilt thou let it
    Slip useless away?

                                                        B

2 GARDEN. (10. 10.)

In moderate time.

Adapted from an
English Traditional Melody.

(*Copyright, 1929, by Oxford University Press.*)

Song of the Dawn. *Based on Robert Herrick, 1591–1674.*

WHEN virgin morn doth call thee to arise,
Come thus in sober joy to sacrifice:

2 First wash thy hands in innocence, then bring
Pure hands, pure habits; make pure every thing.

3 Next humbly kneel before God's throne, and thence
Give up thy soul in clouds of frankincense.

4. Censers of gold, thus filled with odours sweet,
Shall make thy actions with their ends to meet.

3° ST. BOTOLPH. (C.M.)

In moderate time.

GORDON SLATER.

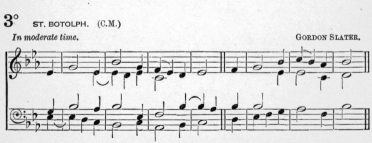

MORNING

Morning.   G. W. B.

DEAR Father, keep me through this day
    Obedient, kind and true:
That, always loving thee, I may
    Seek all thy will to do.

4° MORNING HYMN. (L.M.)

In moderate time.   F. H. BARTHÉLÉMON, 1741–1808.

Morning.   *Rebecca J. Weston.*

FATHER, we thank thee for the night,
    And for the pleasant morning light,
For rest and food and loving care,
And all that makes the day so fair.

2. Help us to do the things we should,
    To be to others kind and good,
    In all we do at work or play
    To grow more loving every day.

3

5° HORSHAM. (77. 77.)

Slow.   English Traditional Melody.

Morning.   *W. Canton, 1845–1926.*

THROUGH the night thy Angels kept
Watch beside me while I slept;
Now the dark has passed away,
Thank thee, Lord, for this new day.

2 North and south and east and west
May thy holy name be blest;
Everywhere beneath the sun,
As in heaven, thy will be done.

3. Give me food that I may live;
Every naughtiness forgive;
Keep all evil things away
From thy little child this day.

(Verse 2 is suitable for a Doxology.)

A - men.

MORNING OR EVENING

6° VOLLER WUNDER. (7 7. 7 7. 7 7.)

In moderate time.

J. G. EBELING, 1620–76.

Morning or Evening.

F. T. Palgrave, 1824–97.

THOU who once on mother's knee
Wast a little one like me,
When I wake, or go to bed,
Lay thy hands upon my head;
Let me feel thee very near,
Jesus Christ, our Saviour dear.

2. Be beside me in the light,
Be close by me through the night;
Make me gentle, kind, and true,
Do what I am bid to do;
Help and cheer me when I fret,
And forgive when I forget.

7 TALLIS' CANON. (L.M.)

Slow and dignified.

T. TALLIS, *c.* 1515–85.

Evening.

Bishop T. Ken, 1637–1711.

GLORY to thee, my God, this night
For all the blessings of the light ;
Keep me, O keep me, King of kings,
Beneath thine own almighty wings.

2 Forgive me, Lord, for thy dear Son,
The ill that I this day have done,
That with the world, myself, and thee,
I, ere I sleep, at peace may be.

3 O may my soul on thee repose,
And with sweet sleep mine eyelids close,
Sleep that may me more vigorous make
To serve my God when I awake.

4. Praise God, from whom all blessings flow,
Praise him, all creatures here below,
Praise him above, ye heavenly host,
Praise Father, Son, and Holy Ghost.

A - men.

8° SHIPSTON. (87. 87.)

In moderate time.

English Traditional Melody.

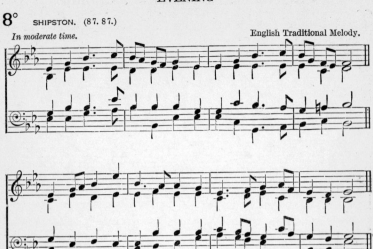

Evening.

Mary L. Duncan, 1814–40.

JESUS, tender Shepherd, hear me,
   Bless thy little lamb to-night;
Through the darkness be thou near me,
   Watch my sleep till morning light.

2 All this day thy hand has led me,
   And I thank thee for thy care;
Thou hast clothed me, warmed and fed me:
   Listen to my evening prayer.

3. Let my sins be all forgiven,
   Bless the friends I love so well;
Take me, when I die, to heaven,
   Happy there with thee to dwell.

9°   TAVISTOCK.   (Irregular.)

Unison. Slow.   English Traditional Melody.

Evening.   *Old Folk-song.*

MATTHEW, Mark, and Luke, and John,
   Bless the bed that I lie on.
Four angels to my bed,
Two to bottom, two to head,
Two to hear me when I pray,
Two to bear my soul away.

2. God is the branch and I the flower.
   Pray God send me a blessèd hour.
   I go to bed some sleep to take:
   The Lord be with me when I wake.
   Sleep I ever, sleep I never,
   God receive my soul for ever.

10° EUDOXIA. (6 5. 6 5.)

Moderately slow.

S. BARING-GOULD, 1834–1924.

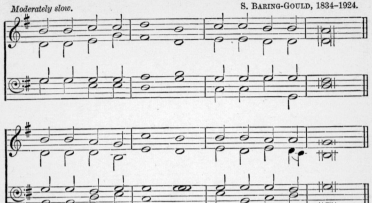

(By permission of A. W. Ridley & Co.)

Evening.

S. *Baring-Gould*, 1834–1924.

NOW the day is over,
  Night is drawing nigh,
Shadows of the evening
  Steal across the sky.

2 Now the darkness gathers,
  Stars begin to peep,
Birds and beasts and flowers
  Soon will be asleep.

3 Jesu, give the weary
  Calm and sweet repose;
With thy tenderest blessing
  May our eyelids close.

4 Grant to little children
  Visions bright of thee;
Guard the sailors tossing
  On the deep blue sea.

5 Comfort every sufferer
  Watching late in pain;
Those who plan some evil
  From their sin restrain.

6 Through the long night watches
  May thine angels spread
Their white wings above me,
  Watching round my bed.

7 When the morning wakens,
  Then may I arise
Pure, and fresh, and sinless
  In thy holy eyes.

8. Glory to the Father,
  Glory to the Son,
And to thee, blest Spirit,
  Whilst all ages run.

A - men.

11 BIRLING. (L.M.)

Not too slow.

From an early 19th cent. MS.

Evening.

J. Keble, 1792–1866.

SUN of my soul, thou Saviour dear,
It is not night if thou be near:
O may no earth-born cloud arise
To hide thee from thy servant's eyes.

2 When the soft dews of kindly sleep
My wearied eyelids gently steep,
Be my last thought, how sweet to rest
For ever on my Saviour's breast.

3*Abide with me from morn till eve,
For without thee I cannot live;
Abide with me when night is nigh,
For without thee I dare not die.

4*If some poor wandering child of thine
Have spurned to-day the voice divine,
Now, Lord, the gracious work begin;
Let him no more lie down in sin.

5 Watch by the sick; enrich the poor
With blessings from thy boundless store;
Be every mourner's sleep to-night
Like infant's slumbers, pure and light.

6. Come near and bless us when we wake,
Ere through the world our way we take;
Till in the ocean of thy love
We lose ourselves in heaven above.

SPRING

G. W. BRIGGS.

Unison. In moderate time.

(*Copyright, 1929, by Oxford University Press.*)

Spring.

G. W. Briggs.

HARK, a hundred notes are swelling
Loud and clear !
'Tis the happy birds are telling
Spring is here !
Nature, decked in brave array,
Casts her winter robes away ;
All earth's little folk rejoicing
Haste to greet the glad new day.

2. Lord and life of all things living,
Come to me :
Thou delightest but in giving ;
Give to me :
Spring of joyous life thou art :
Thine own joy to me impart :
Let my praises be the outburst
Of the Springtime in my heart.

The words in italics may be sung in response : half the voices singing lines 1 and 2, half
singing lines 3 and 4, and all joining in the last four lines of each verse.

13   BAMBERG. (5 5. 4 5. D.)

Moderately quick. Unison.   17th Century Melody, slightly adapted.

The year's at the spring, And day's at the morn;

Morn - ing's at seven; The hill - side's dew - pearled;

The lark's on the wing; The snail's on the thorn;

God's in his heaven— All's right with the world!

Spring.   *Robert Browning, 1812–89.*

THE year's at the spring,
And day's at the morn;
Morning's at seven;
The hill-side's dew-pearled;
The lark's on the wing;
The snail's on the thorn;
God's in his heaven—
All's right with the world!

SUMMER

14 SELMA. (S.M.)

Adapted by R. A. SMITH (1780–1829)
*from a Traditional Melody
of the Isle of Arran.*

In moderate time.

Summer or Harvest.

J. Hampden Gurney, 1802–62.

FAIR waved the golden corn
In Canaan's pleasant land,
When full of joy, some shining morn,
Went forth the reaper-band.

2 To God so good and great
Their cheerful thanks they pour;
Then carry to his temple-gate
The choicest of their store.

3 Like Israel, Lord, we give
Our earliest fruits to thee,
And pray that, long as we shall live,
We may thy children be.

4 Thine is our youthful prime,
And life and all its powers;
Be with us in our morning time,
And bless our evening hours.

5. In wisdom let us grow,
As years and strength are given,
That we may serve thy Church below,
And join thy Saints in heaven.

See also:
78 The holly and the ivy
81 To God who makes all lovely things

15° SUO-GÂN. (6 6. 6 6.)

Rather slowly.

Unison. v. 1.

mp

Welsh Traditional Melody.

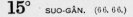

v. 2. (*A little quicker.*)

f

f

(*Copyright, 1929, by Oxford University Press.*)

Winter.   P. D.

WINTER creeps,
Nature sleeps;
Birds are gone,
Flowers are none,
Fields are bare,
Bleak the air,
Leaves are shed:
All seems dead.

2. God's alive!
Grow and thrive,
Hidden away,
Bloom of May,
Robe of June!
Very soon
Nought but green
Will be seen!

14

16 TRURO. (L.M.)

In moderate time.

Psalmodia Evangelica, 1790.

Advent, Epiphany, Ascension.　　　　　*I. Watts,* 1674–1748.

JESUS shall reign where'er the sun
　Does his successive journeys run,
His kingdom stretch from shore to shore,
Till moons shall wax and wane no more.

2 People and realms of every tongue
　Dwell on his love with sweetest song,
　And infant voices shall proclaim
　Their early blessings on his name.

3 Blessings abound where'er he reigns;
　The prisoner leaps to lose his chains;
　The weary find eternal rest,
　And all the sons of want are blest.

4. Let every creature rise and bring
　Peculiar honours to our King;
　Angels descend with songs again,
　And earth repeat the long amen.

17 SANDYS. (S.M. and Refrain.)

English Traditional Melody.

VERSE.

A child this day is born, A child of high re - nown, Most

wor-thy of a scep - tre, A scep-tre and a crown:

CHORUS.

Now - ell, Now - ell, Now - ell, Now - ell, sing all we may, Be-

- cause the King of all kings Was born this bless-ed day.

CHRISTMAS

Christmas.   *Old Carol.*

A CHILD this day is born,
  A child of high renown,
Most worthy of a sceptre,
  A sceptre and a crown:
    Nowell, Nowell, Nowell,
      Nowell, sing all we may,
      Because the King of all kings
      Was born this blessèd day.

2 These tidings shepherds heard,
  In field watching their fold,
Were by an angel unto them
  That night revealed and told:

3 To whom the angel spoke,
  Saying, 'Be not afraid;
Be glad, poor silly shepherds—
  Why are you so dismayed?

4 'For lo! I bring you tidings
  Of gladness and of mirth,
Which cometh to all people by
  This holy infant's birth':

5 Then was there with the angel
  An host incontinent
Of heavenly bright soldiers,
  Which from the Highest was sent:

6 Lauding the Lord our God,
  And his celestial King;
All glory be in Paradise,
  This heavenly host did sing:

7. And as the angel told them,
  So to them did appear;
They found the young child, Jesus Christ,
  With Mary, his mother dear:

('Incontinent' means 'without any delay'.
'Silly' means 'simple'.)

17

18   GOD REST YOU MERRY.   (8 6, 8 6, 8 6, and Refrain.)

Rather quick.   Traditional.

O   tid - ings, O   tid - ings of   com - fort and   joy,

For

CHRISTMAS

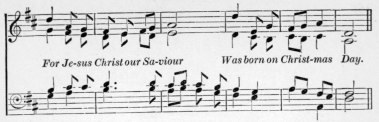

For Je-sus Christ our Sa-viour   Was born on Christ-mas   Day.

Je-sus   Christ   our Sa-viour Was born on   Christ-mas   Day.

Christmas.   *Old Carol.*

GOD rest you merry, Gentlemen,
　Let nothing you dismay,
For Jesus Christ our Saviour
　Was born upon this day,
To save us all from Satan's power
　When we were gone astray:
　　O tidings of comfort and joy,
　　For Jesus Christ our Saviour
　　Was born on Christmas Day.

2 In Bethlehem in Jewry
　　This blessèd babe was born,
And laid within a manger,
　Upon this blessèd morn;
The which his mother Mary
　Nothing did take in scorn:

3 From God our heavenly Father
　A blessèd angel came,
And unto certain shepherds
　Brought tidings of the same,
How that in Bethlehem was born
　The Son of God by name:

4 'Fear not,' then said the angel,
　'Let nothing you affright,
This day is born a Saviour,
　Of virtue, power, and might;
So frequently to vanquish all
　The friends of Satan quite':

5 The shepherds at those tidings
　Rejoicèd much in mind,
And left their flocks a-feeding,
　In tempest, storm and wind,
And went to Bethlehem straightway
　This blessèd babe to find:

6 But when to Bethlehem they came,
　Whereat this infant lay,
They found him in a manger,
　Where oxen feed on hay;
His mother Mary kneeling,
　Unto the Lord did pray:

7. Now to the Lord sing praises,
　All you within this place,
And with true love and brotherhood
　Each other now embrace;
This holy tide of Christmas
　All others doth deface:

('God rest you merry' means 'God keep you merry'.)

19

19°   A LITTLE CHILD. (Irreg.)

In moderate time.

Flemish Traditional,
arr. JULIUS RÖNTGEN.

A lit-tle child on the earth has been born, A lit-tle child on the earth has been born; He came to the earth for the sake of us all, He came to the earth for the sake of us all!

Christmas and New Year.

Old Flemish Carol.
Tr. R. C. Trevelyan.

A LITTLE child on the earth has been born;
He came to the earth for the sake of us all!

2 He came to earth but no home did he find,
   He came to earth and its cross did he bear.

3. He came to earth for the sake of us all
   And wishes us all a happy New Year.

CHRISTMAS

20° I SAW THREE SHIPS. (Irreg.)

Rather quick.

English Traditional Melody.

Christmas.

Old Carol.

I SAW three ships come sailing in,
On Christmas Day, on Christmas Day,
I saw three ships come sailing in,
On Christmas Day in the morning.

2 And what was in those ships all three?

3 Our Saviour Christ and his lady.

4 Pray, whither sailed those ships all three?

5 O, they sailed into Bethlehem.

6 And all the bells on earth shall ring,

7 And all the angels in Heaven shall sing,

8 And all the souls on earth shall sing.

9. Then let us all rejoice amain!

21 ADESTE FIDELES. (Irreg.)

Very slow.

Composer unknown. Probably 18th cent.

Without pedals.

Pedals.

Christmas, Epiphany.   *18th cent.*

O COME, all ye faithful,
    Joyful and triumphant,
O come ye, O come ye to Bethlehem;
    Come and behold him
    Born the King of Angels:
        O come, let us adore him,
        O come, let us adore him,
    O come, let us adore him, Christ the Lord!

2*   God of God,
        Light of Light,
  Lo! he abhors not the Virgin's womb;
        Very God,
        Begotten, not created:

3*   See how the Shepherds,
        Summoned to his cradle,
  Leaving their flocks, draw nigh with lowly fear;
        We too will thither
        Bend our joyful footsteps:

4*   Lo! star-led chieftains,
        Magi, Christ adoring,
Offer him incense, gold, and myrrh;
        We to the Christ Child
        Bring our hearts' oblations:

Part 2

5   Child, for us sinners
        Poor and in the manger,
Fain we embrace thee, with awe and love;
        Who would not love thee,
        Loving us so dearly?

6   Sing, choirs of Angels,
        Sing in exultation,
Sing, all ye citizens of heaven above;
        Glory to God
        In the Highest:

7.*   Yea, Lord, we greet thee,
        Born this happy morning,
Jesu, to thee be glory given;
        Word of the Father,
        Now in flesh appearing:

A - men.

Part 2 (with or without verse 1) makes a short hymn, and verse 7 may be omitted. Verse 4 is useful on and after the Epiphany. The whole hymn makes a fine processional.

22 THE FIRST NOWELL, (Irreg.)

In moderate time.

English Traditional Melody.

REFRAIN.

* It is suggested that the organ remain silent until the Refrain in one or more verses.

EPIPHANY, CHRISTMAS

Epiphany, Christmas.   *Old Carol.*

THE first Nowell the angel did say
  Was to certain poor shepherds in fields as they lay;
In fields where they lay, keeping their sheep,
In a cold winter's night that was so deep:
  Nowell, Nowell, Nowell, Nowell,
  Born is the King of Israel !

2*They lookèd up and saw a star,
  Shining in the east, beyond them far;
  And to the earth it gave great light,
  And so it continued both day and night:

3 And by the light of that same star,
  Three Wise Men came from country far;
  To seek for a king was their intent,
  And to follow the star wheresoever it went:

4 This star drew nigh to the north-west;
  O'er Bethlehem it took its rest,
  And there it did both stop and stay
  Right over the place where Jesus lay:

Part 2

5*Then did they know assuredly
  Within that house the King did lie:
  One entered in then for to see,
  And found the babe in poverty:

6 Then entered in those Wise Men three,
  Fell reverently upon their knee,
  And offered there in his presence
  Both gold and myrrh and frankincense:

7*Between an ox-stall and an ass
  This child truly there born he was;
  For want of clothing they did him lay
  All in the manger, among the hay:

8 Then let us all with one accord
  Sing praises to our heavenly Lord,
  That hath made heaven and earth of naught,
  And with his blood mankind hath bought:

9.*If we in our time shall do well,
  We shall be free from death and hell;
  For God hath preparèd for us all
  A resting place in general:

('*A resting place in general*' means '*A universal resting place*', that is to say a paradise for all.)

23 RODMELL. (C.M.)

In moderate time.

English Traditional Melody.

Christmas, Innocents.

L. Housman.

WHEN Christ was born in
Bethlehem,
  Fair peace on earth to bring,
In lowly state of love he came
  To be the children's King.

2 A mother's heart was there his
throne,
  His orb a maiden's breast,
Whereby he made through love
  His kingdom manifest.   [alone

3 And round him, then, a holy band
  Of children blest was born,
Fair guardians of his throne to stand
  Attendant night and morn.

4 And unto them this grace was given
  A Saviour's name to own,
And die for him who out of heaven
  Had found on earth a throne.

5 O blessèd babes of Bethlehem,
  Who died to save our King,
Ye share the Martyrs' diadem,
  And in their anthem sing!

6 Your lips, on earth that never spake,
  Now sound the eternal word;
And in the courts of love ye make
  Your children's voices heard.

7. Lord Jesus Christ, eternal Child,
  Make thou our childhood thine;
That we with these the meek and mild
  May share the love divine.

CHRISTMAS

24° WINCHESTER OLD. (C.M.)

In moderate time.   First appeared in *Este's Psalter*, 1592.

Christmas.   Nahum Tate, 1652–1715.

WHILE shepherds watched their flocks by night,
    All seated on the ground,
The Angel of the Lord came down,
    And glory shone around.

2 'Fear not,' said he (for mighty dread
    Had seized their troubled mind);
'Glad tidings of great joy I bring
    To you and all mankind.

3 'To you in David's town this day
    Is born of David's line
A Saviour, who is Christ the Lord;
    And this shall be the sign:

4 'The heavenly Babe you there shall find
    To human view displayed,
All meanly wrapped in swathing bands,
    And in a manger laid.'

5 Thus spake the Seraph; and forthwith
    Appeared a shining throng
Of Angels praising God, who thus
    Addressed their joyful song:

6. 'All glory be to God on high,
    And to the earth be peace;
Good-will henceforth from heaven to men
    Begin and never cease.'

A-men.

*Christmas Hymns are suitable all through January.
Nativity Hymns, Nos. 40, 58, 61, 74, 78, 91, are suitable
at any time.*

27

25 AUS DER TIEFE. (77. 77.)

Slow.

Probably by MARTIN HERBST, 1654–81.

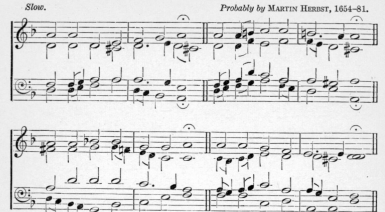

Lent.

G. H. Smyttan ‡, 1825–70.

FORTY days and forty nights
    Thou wast fasting in the wild;
Forty days and forty nights
Tempted still, yet undefiled:

2 Sunbeams scorching all the day,
  Chilly dew-drops nightly shed,
  Prowling beasts about thy way,
  Stones thy pillow, earth thy bed.

3 Shall not we thy sorrow share,
  And from earthly joys abstain,
  With thee watching unto prayer,
  With thee strong to suffer pain?

4*Then if evil on us press,
  Flesh or spirit to assail,
  Victor in the Wilderness,
  Help us not to swerve or fail!

5 So shall we have peace divine;
  Holier gladness ours shall be;
  Round us too shall angels shine,
  Such as ministered to thee.

6. Keep, O keep us, Saviour dear,
   Ever constant by thy side,
   That with thee we may appear
   At the eternal Eastertide.

PALM SUNDAY

26 ST. THEODULPH (VALET WILL ICH DIR GEBEN). (76. 76. D.)

Melody by M. TESCHNER, c. 1613. Adapted
and harmonized by J. S. BACH.

Palm Sunday.

St. Theodulph, c. 820.
Tr. J. M. Neale.

ALL glory, laud, and honour
To thee, Redeemer, King,
To whom the lips of children
Made sweet hosannas ring.

2 Thou art the King of Israel,
Thou David's royal Son,
Who in the Lord's name comest,
The King and blessèd One.

3 The company of Angels
Are praising thee on high,
And mortal men and all things
Created make reply.

4 The people of the Hebrews
With palms before thee went;
Our praise and prayer and anthems
Before thee we present.

5 To thee before thy passion
They sang their hymns of praise;
To thee now high exalted
Our melody we raise.

6. Thou didst accept their praises,
Accept the prayers we bring,
Who in all good delightest,
Thou good and gracious King.

29

27 COME, FAITHFUL PEOPLE. (8 8. 8 7.)

Moderately fast.

Melody by C. BICKNELL, *c.* 1860.

Palm Sunday.

G. Moultrie ‡, 1829–85.

COME, faithful people, come away,
Your homage to your Monarch pay;
It is the feast of palms to-day:
Hosanna in the highest !

2 When Christ, the Lord of all, drew nigh
On Sunday morn to Bethany,
He called two loved ones standing by:

3 'To yonder village go,' said he,
'And there an ass tied up you'll see,
Loose it and bring it unto me':

4 'If any man dispute your word,
Say, "This is needed by the Lord,"
And he permission will accord':

5 The two upon their errand sped,
And found the ass as he had said,
And brought it, then their clothes they spread:

6 They set him on his throne so rude;
Before him went the multitude,
And in the way their garments strewed:

7*Go, Saviour, thus to triumph borne,
Thy crown shall be the wreath of thorn,
Thy royal garb the robe of scorn:

8*They thronged before, behind, around,
They cast palm-branches on the ground,
And still rose up the joyful sound:

HOLY WEEK

9*'Blessèd is Israel's King,' they cry;
    'Blessèd is he that cometh nigh
In name of God the Lord most high':

10. Thus, Saviour, to thy Passion go,
    Arrayed in royalty of woe,
    Assumed for sinners here below:

28° HORSLEY. (C.M.)

Moderately slow.   W. HORSLEY, 1774–1858.

Holy Week.   *Mrs. C. F. Alexander, 1823–95.*

THERE is a green hill far away,
    Without a city wall,
Where the dear Lord was crucified
    Who died to save us all.

2 We may not know, we cannot tell,
    What pains he had to bear,
But we believe it was for us
    He hung and suffered there.

3 He died that we might be forgiven,
    He died to make us good;
That we might go at last to heaven,
    Saved by his precious blood.

4. O, dearly, dearly has he loved,
    And we must love him too,
And trust in his redeeming blood,
    And try his works to do.

31

29   BRIDGWATER.   (64. 63. D.)

In moderate time.

Adapted from an
English Traditional Melody.

LANGPORT.   (64. 63. D.)

In moderate time.

Adapted from an
English Traditional Melody.

Story of the Cross   *M. D.*

The Question.

SEE him in raiment rent,
  With his blood dyed:
Women walk sorrowing
              by his side.

2 Multitudes hurrying
    Pass on the road:
  Simon is called to help
              with the load.

3 Who is this travelling
    With the grim tree—
  This weary prisoner—
              who is he?

The Answer.

4 Follow to Calvary,
    Tread where he trod:
  This is the Lord of life—
              Son of God.

5 Is there no loveliness—
    You who pass by—
  In that lone Figure which
              marks the sky?

6 You who would love him, stand,
    Gaze at his face;
  Noble in gentleness,
              full of grace.

The Cross.

7 On the cross lifted up,
    Thy face I scan,
  Scarred by that agony—
              Son of Man.

8 Thorns form thy diadem,
    Rough wood thy throne;
  Three helpless women there
              sob and moan.

9 Nails hold thy hands and feet,
    While on thy breast
  Sinketh thy bleeding head
              sore opprest.

10 Loud is thy bitter cry,
    Dark is the day;
  Quailing disciples hide
              far away.

11 What, O my Saviour dear,
    What didst thou see,
  That made thee suffer and
              die for me?

The Message of the Cross.

12 Child of my grief and pain!
    From realms above,
  I came to lead thee to
              life and love.

13 For thee my blood I shed,
    For thee I died:
  Safe in my faithfulness
              now abide.

14 I saw thee wandering,
    Weak and at strife;
  I am the Way for thee,
              Truth, and Life.

15 Follow my path of pain,
    Tread where I trod:
  This is the way of peace
              up to God.

The Resolve.

16 O I will follow thee,
    Star of my soul!
  Through the great dark I press
              to the goal.

17 Yea, let me know thy grief,
    Carry thy cross,
  Share in thy sacrifice,
              gain thy loss.

18 Daily I'll prove my love
    Through joy and woe;
  Where thy hands point the way,
              there I go.

19. Lead me on year by year,
      Safe to the end,
  Jesu, my Lord, my Life,
              King, and Friend.

See also :
  64 It is a thing most wonderful
  93 Who within that stable

30 EASTER HYMN. (74. 74. D.)

Slow.

Altered from melody in *Lyra Davidica*, 1708.

Easter.

1708, 1816.

JESUS Christ is risen to-day,   *Alleluya !*
 Our triumphant holy day,   *Alleluya !*
Who did once, upon the cross,   *Alleluya !*
Suffer to redeem our loss.   *Alleluya !*

2 Hymns of praise then let us sing
 Unto Christ, our heavenly King,
 Who endured the cross and grave,
 Sinners to redeem and save.

3. But the pains that he endured
 Our salvation have procured ;
 Now above the sky he 's King,
 Where the angels ever sing.

31 CHEERFUL. (C.M.)

Moderately fast.

MARTIN SHAW.

Org.

(*Copyright*, 1915, *by J. Curwen & Sons, Ltd.*)

Easter, Ascension, etc.   *I. Watts*, 1674–1748.

COME, let us join our cheerful songs
  With angels round the throne;
Ten thousand thousand are their tongues,
  But all their joys are one.

2 'Worthy the Lamb that died,' they cry,
  'To be exalted thus';
'Worthy the Lamb,' our lips reply,
  'For he was slain for us.'

3 Jesus is worthy to receive
  Honour and power divine;
And blessings more than we can give
  Be, Lord, for ever thine.

4. The whole creation join in one
  To bless the sacred name
Of him that sits upon the throne,
  And to adore the Lamb.

For Easter, Ascension, and other festivals, see:

  16 Jesus shall reign
  51 God is love
  53 God my Father, loving me
  65 Jesu, good
  67 Let all the world
  77 The first good joy
  90 When Jesus was a baby
  93 Who within that stable
  102 Praise him, praise him
  109 O mother dear, Jerusalem

Also see THANKSGIVING AND PRAISE.

32 ST. EDMUND. (S.M.)

Moderately slow.

Adapted from Hymn Melody by
E. GILDING, *d.* 1782.

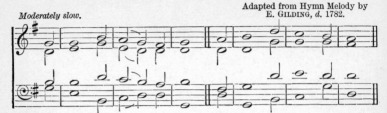

The Eternal Spirit. P. D.

O HOLY Spirit, God,
  All loveliness is thine;
Geat things and small are all in thee,
  The star-world is thy shrine.

2 The sunshine thou of God,
  The life of man and flower,
The wisdom and the energy
  That fills the world with power.

3 Thou art the stream of love
  The unity divine;
Good men and true are one in thee,
  And in thy radiance shine.

4 The heroes and the saints
  Thy messengers became; [world
And all the lamps that guide the
  Were kindled at thy flame.

5 The calls that come to us
  Upon thy winds are brought;
The light that gleams beyond our dreams
  Is something thou hast thought.

6. Give fellowship, we pray,
  In love and joy and peace,
That we in counsel, knowledge, might,
  And wisdom, may increase.

(For Doxology see No. 113.)

See also:

92 Who has seen the wind

For Trinity Sunday see especially:
    51 God is love
    54 God who made the earth
    67 Let all the world in every corner sing
    102 Praise him, praise him

ANGELS

33 SOLOTHURN. (L.M.)

In moderate time. Unison.

Swiss Traditional Melody.

Angels.

J. M. Neale, 1818–66.

AROUND the throne of God a band
Of glorious Angels always stand;
Bright things they see, sweet harps they hold,
And on their heads are crowns of gold.

2 Some wait around him, ready still
To sing his praise and do his will;
And some, when he commands them, go
To guard his servants here below.

3 Lord, give thy Angels every day
Command to guide us on our way,
And bid them every evening keep
Their watch around us while we sleep.

4. So shall no wicked thing draw near,
To do us harm or cause us fear;
And we shall dwell, when life is past,
With Angels round thy throne at last.

34 MOUNT EPHRAIM. (S.M.)

Slow.

B. MILGROVE, 1731–1810.

Saints.

Bishop R. Mant, 1776–1848.

FOR all thy Saints, O Lord,
   Who strove in thee to live,
Who followed thee, obeyed, adored,
   Our grateful hymn receive.

2   For all thy Saints, O Lord,
      Accept our thankful cry,
  Who counted thee their great reward,
      And strove in thee to die.

3   They all in life and death,
      With thee their Lord in view,
  Learnt from thy Holy Spirit's breath
      To suffer and to do.

4.   For this thy name we bless,
      And humbly beg that we
  May follow them in holiness,
      And live and die in thee.

(*In the first verse, 'For this thy Saint, O Lord' may be substituted.*)

35 ST. ANNE. (C.M.)

Slow and dignified.

Melody from the *Supplement to
the New Version*, 1708. Probably
by W. CROFT, 1671–1727.

MARTYRS

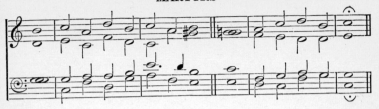

Martyrs, &c.

Bishop R. Heber, 1783–1826.

THE Son of God goes forth to war,
  A kingly crown to gain;
His blood-red banner streams afar!
  Who follows in his train?

2 Who best can drink his cup of woe,
    Triumphant over pain,
  Who patient bears his cross below,
    He follows in his train.

Part 2

3*The Martyr first, whose eagle eye
    Could pierce beyond the grave;
  Who saw his Master in the sky,
    And called on him to save.

4*Like him, with pardon on his tongue
    In midst of mortal pain,
  He prayed for them that did the
    wrong!
  Who follows in his train?

5*A glorious band, the chosen few
    On whom the Spirit came,
  Twelve valiant Saints, their hope
    they knew,
  And mocked the cross and flame.

6*They met the tyrant's brandish'd
    steel,
  The lion's gory mane,   [feel;
  They bowed their necks the death to
  Who follows in their train?

Part 3

7 A noble army, men and boys,
    The matron and the maid,
  Around the Saviour's throne rejoice
    In robes of light arrayed.

8. They climbed the steep ascent of heaven
    Through peril, toil, and pain;
  O God, to us may grace be given
    To follow in their train.

(*Verses 3 and 4 refer to St. Stephen: they can be omitted,
and the Apostles' verse 5 also: verse 6 can be used for
Martyrs as well as Apostles, or omitted. Parts 1 and 3
make a good hymn. 'Brandished steel' means a sword
waved in the air.*)

For the Saints see also:
        32 O Holy Spirit, God
        109 Part 3, Thy Saints are crowned

PART II
GENERAL HYMNS

36 NUN LASST UNS GOTT DEM HERREN. (77. 77.)

In moderate time.

Later form of melody in
Selneccer's *Christliche Psalmen*, 1587.

Resurrection.

P. D.

A BRIGHTER dawn is breaking,
  And earth with praise is waking;
For thou, O King most highest,
The power of death defiest;

2 And thou hast come victorious,
With risen body glorious,
Who now for ever livest,
And life abundant givest.

3 O free the world from blindness,
And fill the world with kindness,
Give sinners resurrection,
Bring striving to perfection;

4. In sickness give us healing,
In doubt thy clear revealing,
That praise to thee be given
In earth as in thy heaven.

GENERAL

37 OLD HUNDREDTH. (L.M.)

Melody from *Genevan Psalter*, 1551
(English form of final line).

Slow and dignified.

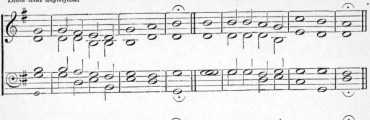

Ps. 100.   *Daye's Psalter* (1560–1).

A<small>LL</small> people that on earth do dwell,
    Sing to the Lord with cheerful voice;
Him serve with fear, his praise forth tell,
    Come ye before him, and rejoice.

2 The Lord, ye know, is God indeed,
    Without our aid he did us make;
We are his folk, he doth us feed,
    And for his sheep he doth us take.

3 O enter then his gates with praise,
    Approach with joy his courts unto;
Praise, laud, and bless his name always,
    For it is seemly so to do.

4 For why? the Lord our God is good:
    His mercy is for ever sure;
His truth at all times firmly stood,
    And shall from age to age endure.

5. To Father, Son, and Holy Ghost,
    The God whom heaven and earth adore,
From men and from the angel-host
    Be praise and glory evermore.

*(This is called 'The Old Hundredth', because it is the old
version of the Hundredth Psalm. It was written, with its
music as we have it, in the reign of Queen Elizabeth.)*

A - men.

38° ROYAL OAK. (76. 76. and refrain.)

Fast. Voices in Unison.

Arranged by MARTIN SHAW
from an English Traditional Melody.

1. *All things bright and beau-ti-ful, All crea-tures great and small, All things wise and won-der-ful, The Lord God made them all.*

FINE.

2. Each lit-tle flower that

D.C.

NOTE.—*The pause* (⌢) *is for the last time only.*

Mrs. C. F. Alexander ‡, 1823–95.

ALL things bright and beautiful,
All creatures great and small,
All things wise and wonderful,
The Lord God made them all.

2 Each little flower that opens,
   Each little bird that sings,
He made their glowing colours,
   He made their tiny wings:

3 The purple-headed mountain,
   The river running by,
The sunset and the morning,
   That brightens up the sky:

4 The cold wind in the winter,
   The pleasant summer sun,
The ripe fruits in the garden—
   He made them every one:

5 The tall trees in the greenwood,
   The meadows for our play,
The rushes by the water,
   To gather every day:

6. He gave us eyes to see them,
   And lips that we might tell
How great is God Almighty,
   Who has made all things well:

39 EVAN. (C.M.)

W. H. HAVERGAL, 1793–1870.
(Original time ½)

In moderate time.

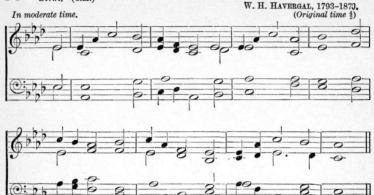

Edward John Brailsford, 1841–1921.

ALL things which live below the sky,
   Or move within the sea,
Are creatures of the Lord most High,
   And brothers unto me.

2 I love to hear the robin sing,
   Perched on the highest bough;
To see the rook with purple wing
   Follow the shining plough.

3 I love to watch the swallow skim
   The river in his flight;
To mark, when day is growing dim,
   The glow-worm's silvery light;

4 The sea-gull whiter than the foam,
   The fish that dart beneath;
The lowing cattle coming home;
   The goats upon the heath.

5 God taught the wren to build her nest,
   The lark to soar above,
The hen to gather to her breast
   The offspring of her love.

6 Beneath his heaven there's room for all;
   He gives to all their meat;
He sees the meanest sparrow fall
   Unnoticed in the street.

7. Almighty Father, King of kings,
   The Lover of the meek,
Make me a friend of helpless things,
   Defender of the weak.

40 CHERRY. (76. 76.)

In moderate time.

English Traditional Melody.

Nativity.

From the Cherry Tree Carol.

A S Joseph was a-walking,
He heard an angel sing:
'This night there shall be born
On earth our heavenly King;

2 'He neither shall be born
In housen nor in hall,
Nor in the place of Paradise,
But in an ox's stall.

3 'He neither shall be clothèd
In purple nor in pall,
But all in fair linen
As wear the babies all.

4 'He neither shall be rockèd
In silver nor in gold,
But in a wooden cradle
That rocks upon the mould.

5. 'He neither shall be christened
In white wine nor red,
But with fair spring water
As we were christenèd.'

41 GALLIARD. (77. 77.)

In moderate time.

Adapted from a Melody
by J. DOWLAND, 1563–1626.

(*Copyright, 1925, by Martin Shaw.*)

William Blake, 1757–1827.

CAN I see another's woe,
And not be in sorrow too?
Can I see another's grief,
And not seek for kind relief?

2 Can I see a falling tear,
And not feel my sorrow's share?
Can a father see his child
Weep, nor be with sorrow filled?

3 God doth give his joy to all;
He becomes an infant small,
He becomes a man of woe,
He doth feel the sorrow too.

4 Think not thou canst sigh a sigh,
And thy Maker is not by;
Think not thou canst weep a tear,
And thy Maker is not near.

5. O! he gives to us his joy
That our grief he may destroy:
Till our grief is fled and gone,
He doth sit by us and moan.

42°   TREFAENAN.   (87. 87. 887.)

Not too quick.

Welsh Traditional Melody.

He hath made them, He hath made them, He hath made them, ev - ery one.
And he loves them, And he loves them, And he loves them, ev - ery one.

(*Copyright, 1929, by Oxford University Press.*)

E. M. Arndt, 1769–1860.
Tr. H. W. Dulcken ‡.

CAN you count the stars that brightly
    Twinkle in the midnight sky?
Can you count the clouds, so lightly
    O'er the meadows floating by?
God, the Lord, doth mark their number
With his eyes that never slumber;
    He hath made them, every one.

2. Do you know how many children
    Rise each morning blithe and gay?
Can you count their jolly voices,
    Singing sweetly day by day?
God hears all the merry voices,
In their pretty songs rejoices;
    And he loves them, every one.

43° FAIRFIELD. (3 8. 6 5. 6 3.)

In moderate time.

G. W. BRIGGS.

(Copyright, 1929, by Oxford University Press.)

St. Richard of Chichester, c. 1197–1253.

D_{AY by day,}
Dear Lord, of thee three things I pray:
To see thee more clearly,
Love thee more dearly,
Follow thee more nearly,
Day by day.

44°   NEWLAND.   (6 5. 6 5.)

Brightly.

J. ARMSTRONG (?).

Mrs. C. F. Alexander, 1823–95.

DO no sinful action,
   Speak no angry word;
Ye belong to Jesus,
   Children of the Lord.

2 Christ is kind and gentle,
   Christ is pure and true;
And his little children
   Must be holy too.

3 Ye are new-born Christians,
   Ye must learn to fight
With the bad within you,
   And to do the right.

4. Christ is your own Master,
   He is good and true,
And his little children
   Must be holy too.

E

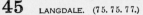

45 LANGDALE. (7 5. 7 5. 7 7.)

A. SOMERVELL.

In moderate time.

Mrs. C. F. Alexander, 1823–95.

EVERY morning the red sun
  Rises warm and bright;
But the evening cometh on,
  And the dark, cold night.
There's a bright land far away,
Where 'tis never-ending day.

2 Every spring the sweet young flowers
  Open bright and gay,
Till the chilly autumn hours
  Wither them away.
There's a land we have not seen,
Where the trees are always green.

3 Little birds sing songs of praise
  All the summer long,
But in colder, shorter days
  They forget their song.
There's a place where Angels sing
Ceaseless praises to their King.

4 Christ our Lord is ever near
  Those who follow him;
But we cannot see him here,
  For our eyes are dim;
There is a most happy place,
Where men always see his face.

5. Who shall go to that bright land?
  All who do the right:
Holy children there shall stand
  In their robes of white;
For that heaven, so bright and blest,
Is our everlasting rest.

46 GUN HILL. (55.65.87.87.)

In moderate time.

MARTIN SHAW.

(Copyright, 1929, by Oxford University Press.)

S. P. from Goethe.

EVERYTHING changes
But One changes not;
The power never changes
That lies in his thought:
Sisters three, from God proceeding,
May we ever love them true,
Goodness, Truth, and Beauty heeding
Every day, in all we do.

2 Truth never changes,
    And Beauty's its dress,
And Good never changes,
    Which those two express:

3 Perfect together
    And lovely apart,

These three cannot wither;
    They spring from God's heart:

4. Some things are screening
    God's glory below;
But this is the meaning
    Of all that we know:

47° THE BIRDS. (10 2. 10 2. 8 8 6.)

Czech Traditional Carol.

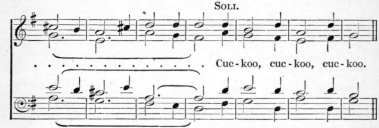

(*Copyright*, 1928, *by Martin Shaw*.)

The Birds Carol.

P. D. from the Czech.

FROM out of a wood did a cuckoo fly,
    Cuckoo,
He came to a manger with joyful cry,
    Cuckoo ;   [flew,
He hopped, he curtsied, round he
And loud his jubilation grew,
    Cuckoo, cuckoo, cuckoo.

2 A pigeon flew over to Galilee,
    Vrercroo,   [of glee,
He strutted, and cooed, and was full
    Vrercroo,

And showed with jewelled wings
    unfurled,
His joy that Christ was in the world,
    Vrercroo, Vrercroo, Vrercroo.

3. A dove settled down upon Nazareth,
    Tsucroo,
And tenderly chanted with all his
    breath,
    Tsucroo:
'O you,' he cooed, 'so good and true,
My beauty do I give to you—
    Tsucroo, Tsucroo, Tsucroo.'

52

48° GENTLE JESUS. (77. 77.)

MARTIN SHAW.

In moderate time.

C. Wesley, 1707–88.

GENTLE Jesus, meek and mild,
Look upon a little child;
Pity my simplicity,
Suffer me to come to thee.

2 Fain I would to thee be brought,
Dearest God, forbid it not;
Give me, dearest God, a place
In the kingdom of thy grace.

Part 2.

3 Lamb of God, I look to thee;
Thou shalt my example be:
Thou art gentle, meek and mild,
Thou wast once a little child.

4 Fain I would be as thou art;
Give me thy obedient heart.
Thou art pitiful and kind,
Let me have thy loving mind.

5 Let me, above all, fulfil
God my heavenly Father's will,
Never his good Spirit grieve,
Only to his glory live.

Part 3.

6 Thou didst live to God alone;
Thou didst never seek thine own;
Thou thyself didst never please:
God was all thy happiness.

7 Loving Jesus, gentle Lamb,
In thy gracious hands I am:
Make me, Saviour, what thou art;
Live thyself within my heart.

8. I shall then show forth thy praise,
Serve thee all my happy days;
Then the world shall always see
Christ, the holy Child, in me.

49° WATER-END. (65. 65. Irregular.)

Brightly. Voices in Unison.   GEOFFREY SHAW.

Glad that I live am I; That the sky is blue;

simile.

Glad for the coun-try lanes, And the fall of dew.

2 Af - ter the sun the rain, Af - ter the rain the sun;

This is the way of life, Till the work be done.

3. All that we need to do, Be we low or high, Is to see that we grow Near-er . . the sky.

(*Copyright, 1925, by Oxford University Press.*)

Lizette Woodworth Reese.

First tune.

50 CONSTANTIA. (Irregular.)

Moderately slow.

R. O. MORRIS.

1 God be in my head, And in my un-der-stand-ing; 2 God be in mine

eyes, And in my look-ing; 3 God be in my mouth, And in my

speak-ing; 4 God be in my heart, And in my think-ing;

5. God be at mine end, And at my de-part-ing.

GENERAL

Second tune.

DAVID. (Irregular.)

Rather slow.

G. W. BRIGGS.

1 God be in my head, And in my un-der-stand-ing;

2 God be in mine eyes, And in my look-ing; 3 God be in my

mouth, And in my speak-ing; 4 God be in my heart, And in my

Rather more slowly and quietly. rall. . . . .

think-ing; 5. God be at mine end, And at my de-part-ing.

(*Copyright, 1929, by Oxford University Press.*)

Sarum Primer, 1558.

The pronoun can be changed to 'your' if you want to sing it for some one else—at a baptism or on a birthday, for instance.

57

51° THEODORIC. (6 6 6. 6 6. 5 5. 3 9.)

In moderate time.

Melody from *Piae Cantiones*, 1582.
Arr. by GUSTAV HOLST.

God is love, his the care,
Tend-ing all ev-'ry-where, God is love— all is there!
Je-sus came to show him, That we all may know him:

GENERAL

Sing a - loud, loud, loud! Sing a - loud, loud, loud!

God is good! God is truth! God is beau-ty! Praise him!

(Copyright, 1924, by Gustav Holst.)

P. D.

2 None can see God above,
All have here man to love;
Thus may we Godward move,
   Finding him in others,
   Holding all men brothers:

3 Jesus lived here for men,
Strove and died, rose again,
Rules our hearts, now as then;
   For he came to save us
   By the truth he gave us:

4. To our Lord praise we sing—
Light and Life, Friend and King,
Coming down love to bring,
   Pattern for our duty,
   Showing God in beauty:

52° GLENFINLAS. (65. 65.)

Unison.

K. G. FINLAY.

Robin.

Florence Hoatson.

GOD made little Robin
  In the days of Spring.
'Please,' said little Robin,
  'When am I to sing?'

2 God then spoke to Robin:
  'You must sing always,
But your sweetest carol
  Keep for wintry days!'

3 God heard Robin singing
  Such a welcome song,
'Cheer up, little children!
  Summer won't be long!'

4. God loves all the children,
  And it makes him glad
If they sing like Robin
  When the days are sad.

53° ST. JOAN. (7 7. 7 7.)

In moderate time.

G. W. BRIGGS.

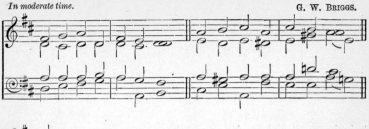

(*Copyright*, 1929, *by Oxford University Press.*)

G. W. Briggs.

GOD my Father, loving me,
    Gave his Son, my friend to be:
Gave his Son, my form to take,
    And to suffer for my sake.

2 Jesus still remains the same
    As in days of old he came:
As my Brother by my side,
    Still he seeks my steps to guide.

3 How can I repay thy love,
    Lord of all the hosts above?
What have I, a child, to bring
    Unto thee, thou heavenly King?

4 I have but myself to give:
    Let me to thy glory live:
Let me follow, day by day,
    Thee, the true and living Way.

5. Then, when I am called to share
    Yonder home thou dost prepare,
I shall meet my King, and praise
    Him through everlasting days.

54°   HERMITAGE.   (5 6. 6 4.)

In moderate time.   Unison.

EVELYN SHARPE.

(*Copyright*, 1929, *by Oxford University Press.*)

Sarah Betts Rhodes (1870).

GOD who made the earth,
    The air, the sky, the sea,
Who gave the light its birth,
     Careth for me.

2 God who made the grass,
    The flower, the fruit, the trees,
   The day and night to pass,
     Careth for me.

3. God who made the sun,
    The moon, the stars, is he
   Who when life's clouds come on,
     Careth for me.

55° HASLEMERE. (55.55.)

Old Air.
Arr. by E. R. B.

In moderate time.

Florence Hoatson.

G OD whose name is Love,
   Little ones are we!
Listen to the hymn
   That we sing to thee.

2 Help us to be good,
   Always kind and true,
In the games we play
   Or the work we do.

3. Bless us every one
   Singing here to thee.
God whose name is Love,
   Loving may we be!

56 MONKS GATE. (11 11. 12 11.)

Adapted from an
English Traditional Melody.

Brightly.

J. Bunyan, 1628–88, and others.

HE who would valiant be
   'Gainst all disaster,
Let him in constancy
   Follow the Master.
There's no discouragement
Shall make him once relent
His first avowed intent
   To be a pilgrim.

2 Who so beset him round
   With dismal stories,
Do but themselves confound—
   His strength the more is.
No foes shall stay his might,
Though he with giants fight:
He will make good his right
   To be a pilgrim.

3. Since, Lord, thou dost defend
   Us with thy Spirit,
We know we at the end
   Shall life inherit.
Then fancies flee away!
I'll fear not what men say,
I'll labour night and day
   To be a pilgrim.

57 PLEADING SAVIOUR. (87. 87. D.)

Plymouth Collection (U.S.A.), 1855.

In moderate time. *Fine.*

D.C.

Bishop C. Wordsworth, 1807-85.

HEAVENLY Father, send thy blessing
  On thy children gathered here,
May they all, thy name confessing,
  Be to thee for ever dear;
May they be, like Joseph, loving,
  Dutiful, and chaste, and pure;
And their faith, like David proving,
  Steadfast unto death endure.

2 Holy Saviour, who in meekness
  Didst vouchsafe a Child to be,
Guide their steps, and help their weakness,
  Bless, and make them like to thee;
Bear thy lambs when they are weary,
  In thine arms, and at thy breast;
Through life's desert, dry and dreary,
  Bring them to thy heavenly rest.

3. Spread thy golden pinions o'er them,
  Holy Spirit, heavenly Dove,
Guide them, lead them, go before them,
  Give them peace, and joy, and love;
Temples of the Holy Spirit,
  May they with thy glory shine,
And immortal bliss inherit,
  And for evermore be thine!

58° STOWEY. (74. 74. Irregular.)

In moderate time. Voices in unison.

Adapted from an
English Traditional Melody.

1 How far is it to Beth - le-hem? Not ve - ry far.

Omit in v. 5.

Shall we find the sta - ble-room Lit by a star?

2 Can we see the lit - tle Child, Is he with - in?

Omit in v. 7.

66

If we lift the wood-en latch May we go in?

Omit in vv. 6 & 7.

Vv. 5 & 6.

5 Great kings have pre - cious gifts, And we have naught,

Lit - tle smiles and lit - tle tears Are all . we brought. 6* For

all wea - ry chil - dren Ma - ry must weep.

Here, on his bed of straw Sleep, chil - dren, sleep.

For v. 7 repeat music of v. 2.

Children's Song of the Nativity.   *Frances Chesterton.*

HOW far is it to Bethlehem?
  Not very far.
Shall we find the stable-room
  Lit by a star?

2 Can we see the little Child,
    Is he within?
  If we lift the wooden latch
    May we go in?

3 May we stroke the creatures there,
    Ox, ass, or sheep?
  May we peep like them and see
    Jesus asleep?

4 If we touch his tiny hand
    Will he awake?
  Will he know we've come so far
    Just for his sake?

5 Great kings have precious gifts,
    And we have naught,
  Little smiles and little tears
    Are all we brought.

6*For all weary children
    Mary must weep.
  Here, on his bed of straw
    Sleep, children, sleep.

7.* God in his mother's arms,
      Babes in the byre,
    Sleep, as they sleep who find
      Their heart's desire.

67

59° ELLACOMBE. (7 6. 7 6. D.)

Brightly.

Mainz Gesangbuch, 1833.

G. W. Briggs.

I LOVE God's tiny creatures
  That wander wild and free,
The crimson-coated lady-bird,
  The velvet humming-bee:
Shy little flowers in hedge and dyke
  That hide themselves away:
God paints them, though they are
    so small,
  God makes them bright and gay.

2. Dear Father, who hast all things
    made,
  And carest for them all, [love,
There's none too great for thy great
  Nor anything too small:
If thou canst spend such tender care
  On things that grow so wild,
How wonderful thy love must be
  For me, thy little child.

60° EAST HORNDON. (Irregular.)

Moderately fast. To be sung in unison. English Traditional Melody.

Mrs. J. Luke, 1813–1906.

I THINK, when I read that sweet story of old,
  When Jesus was here among men,
How he called little children as lambs to his fold,
  I should like to have been with him then.
I wish that his hands had been placed on my head,
  That his arm had been thrown around me,
And that I might have seen his kind look when he said,
  'Let the little ones come unto me.'

2 Yet still to his footstool in prayer I may go,
  And ask for a share in his love;
And if I now earnestly seek him below,
  I shall see him and hear him above:
In that beautiful place he has gone to prepare
  For all who are washed and forgiven.
And many dear children are gathering there,
  'For of such is the kingdom of heaven.'

3. But thousands and thousands who wander and fall
  Never heard of that heavenly home;
I should like them to know there is room for them all,
  And that Jesus has bid them to come.
I long for the joy of that glorious time,
  The sweetest, and brightest, and best,
When the dear little children of every clime
  Shall crowd to his arms and be blest.

61° PEACEFIELD. (7 7. 7 7.)

Ancient Irish Lullaby,
harmonized by DAVID F. R. WILSON.

Rather slow.

Nativity.   *Eleanor Smith.*

IN another land and time,
  Long ago and far away,
Was a little Baby born
  On the first glad Christmas day.

2 Words of truth and deeds of love
    Filled his life from day to day,
  So that all the world was blessed
    On the first glad Christmas day.

3. Little children did he love
    With a tender love alway:
  So should little children be
    Always glad for Christmas day.

62 BELL CAROL. (74. 74. 10. 66.)

In moderate time.

Old French Carol Tune.

ring, do ring,

Bell Carol.

Steuart Wilson.

IN every town and village
  The bells do ring,
O'er woods and grass and tillage,
  Hey ding a ding,
Ringing for joy to start the week
  again,
  And call all Christian men
  To pray and praise and sing.

2 Then pull your ropes with vigour,
  And watch your ways
To thread with strictest rigour
  The noisy maze;
Keep in your heart the fire of youth
  alight,
  That he who rings aright
  May ring in happy days.

3. And we who hear the bells ring
  With all their might,
As they do say the angels sing
  Both day and night,
Praise we the men who built our belfries high
  That music from the sky
  Might sound for our delight.

63 LYNE. (77. 77.)

In moderate time.   *Magdalen Hymns,* 1760 (?).

W. Chatterton Dix, 1837–98.

IN our work, and in our play,
   Jesus, be thou ever near;
Guarding, guiding all the day,
   Keeping in thy holy fear.

2 Thou didst toil, O royal Child,
   In the far-off Holy Land,
Blessing labour undefiled,
   Pure and honest, of the hand.

3 Thou wilt bless our play-hour too,
   If we ask thy succour strong;
Watch o'er all we say or do,
   Hold us back from guilt and wrong.

4. O! how happy thus to spend
   Work and playtime in his sight,
Who that day which shall not end
   Gives to those who do the right.

64 HERONGATE. (L.M.)

In moderate time.   English Traditional Melody.

The Cross.   *Bishop W. W. How,* 1823-97.

IT is a thing most wonderful,
　Almost too wonderful to be,
That God's own Son should come from heaven,
　And die to save a child like me.

2 And yet I know that it is true:
　He chose a poor and humble lot,
And wept, and toiled, and mourned, and died
　For love of those who loved him not.

3 I sometimes think about the cross,
　And shut my eyes, and try to see
The cruel nails and crown of thorns,
　And Jesus crucified for me.

4 But even could I see him die,
　I could but see a little part
Of that great love, which, like a fire,
　Is always burning in his heart.

5. And yet I want to love thee, Lord;
　O light the flame within my heart,
And I will love thee more and more,
　Until I see thee as thou art.

65° QUEM PASTORES LAUDAVERE. (8 8. 87.)

In moderate time.

Melody from a 15th-century
German MS.

P. D.

JESU, good above all other,
Gentle Child of gentle mother,
In a stable born our Brother,
 Give us grace to persevere.

2 Jesu, cradled in a manger,
For us facing every danger,
Living as a homeless stranger,
 Make we thee our King most dear.

3 Jesu, for thy people dying,
Risen Master, death defying,
Lord in heaven, thy grace supplying,
 Keep us to thy presence near.

4 Jesu, who our sorrows bearest,
All our thoughts and hopes thou sharest,
Thou to man the truth declarest;
 Help us all thy truth to hear.

5. Lord, in all our doings guide us;
Pride and hate shall ne'er divide us;
We'll go on with thee beside us,
 And with joy we'll persevere!

66° WESTRIDGE. (8 5. 8 3.)

Not too quick.   MARTIN SHAW.

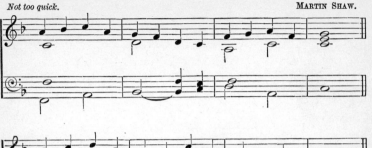

(Copyright, 1929, by Oxford University Press.)

Walter J. Mathams.

JESUS, friend of little children,
  Be a friend to me:
Take my hand, and ever keep me
  Close to thee.

2 Teach me how to grow in goodness,
    Daily as I grow:
  Thou hast been a child, and surely
    Thou dost know.

3. Never leave me, nor forsake me,
    Ever be my friend;
  For I need thee, from life's dawning
    To its end.

67 HIGH ROAD. (10 4. 6 6. 6 6. 10 4.)

Moderately fast.

MARTIN SHAW.

(*Copyright*, 1915, *by J. Curwen & Sons, Ltd.*)

George Herbert, 1593–1632.

LET all the world in every corner sing,
   My God and King!
   The heavens are not too high,
   His praise may thither fly;
   The earth is not too low,
   His praises there may grow.
Let all the world in every corner sing,
   My God and King!

2. Let all the world in every corner sing,
   My God and King!
The Church with psalms must shout,
No door can keep them out;
But above all, the heart
Must bear the longest part.
Let all the world in every corner sing,
   My God and King!

(The first verse may be repeated.)

68°   GOTT EIN VATER.   (65. 65.)

Brightly.
To be sung in unison or in two parts.

F. SILCHER, 1789–1860.
Arranged by W. TSCHIRSCH.

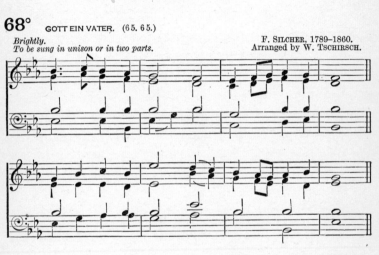

Mrs. J. A. Carney ‡ (1845).

LITTLE drops of water,
    Little grains of sand,
Make the mighty ocean
    And the beauteous land.

2 Little deeds of kindness,
    Little words of love,
Make our earth an Eden,
    Like the heavens above.

3 Little seeds of mercy
    Sown by youthful hands,
Grow to bless the nations
    Far in other lands.

4. Glory then for ever
    Be to God on high,
Beautiful and loving
    To eternity.

69°   EARDISLEY. (C.M.)

In moderate time.   English Traditional Melody.

Jane Taylor, 1783–1824.

LORD, I would own thy tender care,
  And all thy love to me;
The food I eat, the clothes I wear,
  Are all bestowed by thee.

2 'Tis thou preservest me from death
    And dangers every hour;
  I cannot draw another breath
    Unless thou give me power.

3 My health and friends and parents dear
    To me by God are given;
  I have not any blessing here
    But what is sent from heaven.

4. Such goodness, Lord, and constant care,
    A child can ne'er repay;
  But may it be my daily prayer
    To love thee and obey.

70   IL BUON PASTOR.   (87. 877.)

Moderately fast. Unison.   Adapted from a Melody in *Canzuns Spirituaelas*
                                        (Upper Engadine), 1765.

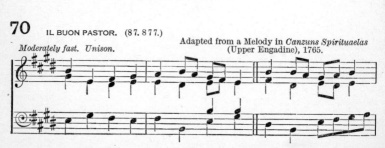

GENERAL

P. D.

LORD of health, thou life within us,
  Strength of all that lives and grows,
Love that meets our hearts to win us,
  Beauty that around us glows,
  Take the praise that brims and flows!

2 Praise for all our work and leisure,
    Mirth and games and jollity,
  Study, science, all the treasure
    That is stored by memory,
    Skill of mind and hand and eye;

3 Praise for joys, for sorrows even,
    All that leads us up to thee;
  Most of all that out from heaven
    Came thy Son to set us free,
    Came to show us what to be.

4. Help us now, each moment filling,
    Keep us true to thee and wise;
  May our work be keen and willing,
    Power and service be our prize—
    Till to thy far hills we rise!

71° INNOCENTS. (7 7. 7 7.)

Composed or adapted by
J. SMITH, 1800–73.

Moderately fast.

Jane E. Leeson, 1807–82.

LOVING Shepherd of thy sheep,
Keep thy lamb, in safety keep;
Nothing can thy power withstand,
None can pluck me from thy hand.

2 Loving Saviour, thou didst give
Thine own life that we might live;
And the hands outstretched to bless
Bear the cruel nails' impress.

3 I would bless thee every day,
Gladly all thy will obey,
Like thy blessèd ones above,
Happy in thy precious love.

4 Loving Shepherd, ever near,
Teach thy lamb thy voice to hear;
Suffer not my steps to stray
From the straight and narrow way.

5. Where thou leadest I would go,
Walking in thy steps below,
Till before my Father's throne
I shall know as I am known.

72° HAMBRIDGE. (76. 76.)

In moderate time.   English Traditional Melody.

A child's own song.   *P. D.*

> O DEAR and lovely Brother,
>   The Son of God alone,
> When we love one another
>   We are thy very own.
>
> 2. In heaven thy face is hidden,
>   Too near for us to see;
>   And each of us is bidden
>   To share that heaven with thee.

73 HARINGTON (RETIREMENT). (C.M.)

Moderately slow.

H. HARINGTON, 1727–1816.

S. T. Coleridge, 1772–1834, and another.

O SWEETER than the marriage-feast,
    'Tis sweeter far to me,
To walk together to the kirk
    With a goodly company!—

2 To walk together to the kirk,
    And all together pray;
Old men and babes and loving friends
    And youths and maidens gay!

3 He prayeth well, who loveth well
    Both man and bird and beast;
And he that loveth all God made,
    That man he prayeth best.

4. He prayeth best, who loveth best
    All things both great and small;
For the dear God who loveth us
    He made and loveth all.

74 IRBY. (87.87.77.)

In moderate time. Unison.

H. J. GAUNTLETT, 1805–76.

Nativity.

Mrs. C. F. Alexander, 1823–95.

ONCE in royal David's city
  Stood a lowly cattle shed,
Where a mother laid her baby
  In a manger for his bed;
Mary was that mother mild,
Jesus Christ her little Child.

2 He came down to earth from heaven,
    Who is God and Lord of all,
  And his shelter was a stable,
    And his cradle was a stall;
  With the poor, and mean, and lowly,
  Lived on earth our Saviour holy.

3 And through all his wondrous child-
      hood
    He would honour and obey,
  Love, and watch the lowly maiden,
    In whose gentle arms he lay;
  Christian children all must be
  Mild, obedient, good as he.

4*For he is our childhood's pattern,
    Day by day like us he grew,
  He was little, weak, and helpless,
    Tears and smiles like us he knew;
  And he feeleth for our sadness,
  And he shareth in our gladness.

5*And our eyes at last shall see him,
    Through his own redeeming love,
  For that child so dear and gentle
    Is our Lord in heaven above;
  And he leads his children on
  To the place where he is gone.

6.*Not in that poor lowly stable,
    With the oxen standing by,
  We shall see him; but in heaven,
    Set at God's right hand on high;
  When like stars his children crowned
  All in white shall wait around.

75° BOYCE. (77. 77.)

Moderately fast. May be sung in unison.

W. BOYCE, 1710–79.

Jane E. Leeson, 1807–82.

SAVIOUR, teach me, day by day,
Love's sweet lesson to obey—
Sweeter lesson cannot be—
Loving him who first loved me.

2 With a child's glad heart of love
At thy bidding may I move,
Prompt to serve and follow thee,
Loving him who first loved me.

3 Teach me thus thy steps to trace,
Strong to follow in thy grace,
Learning how to love from thee,
Loving him who so loved me.

4.*Love in loving finds employ,
In obedience all her joy;
Ever new that joy will be,
Loving him who first loved me.

76° ST. HUGH. (C.M.)

Brightly.

English Traditional Melody.

R. S. Hawker, 1804–73.

SING to the Lord the children's hymn,
  His gentle love declare,
Who bends amid the Seraphim
  To hear the children's prayer.

2 He at a mother's breast was fed,
    Though God's own Son was he;
  He learnt the first small words he said
    At a meek mother's knee.

3 He held us to his mighty breast,
    The children of the earth;
  He lifted up his hands and blessed
    The babes of human birth.

4. Lo! from the stars his face will turn
    On us with glances mild;
  The angels of his presence yearn
    To bless the little child.

77°

JOYS SEVEN. (8 6. 8 6. and refrain.)

Solo or Semi-Chorus.
In moderate time.

English Traditional Tune.

When

CHORUS.

Joys Seven. *Old Carol.*

THE first good joy that Mary had,
It was the joy of one;
To see the blessèd Jesus Christ
When he was first her son:
When he was first her son, good man:

And blessed may he be,
Both Father, Son, and Holy Ghost,
To all eternity.

2 The next good joy that Mary had,
It was the joy of two;
To see her own son, Jesus Christ
To make the lame to go:
To make the lame to go, good man:

3 The next good joy that Mary had,
It was the joy of three;
To see her own son, Jesus Christ
To make the blind to see:
To make the blind to see, good man:

4 The next good joy that Mary had,
It was the joy of four;
To see her own son, Jesus Christ
To read the Bible o'er:
To read the Bible o'er, good man:

5 The next good joy that Mary had,
It was the joy of five;
To see her own son, Jesus Christ
To bring the dead alive:
To bring the dead alive, good man:

6 The next good joy that Mary had,
It was the joy of six;
To see her own son, Jesus Christ
Upon the crucifix:
Upon the crucifix, good man:

7. The next good joy that Mary had,
It was the joy of seven;
To see her own son, Jesus Christ
To wear the crown of heaven:
To wear the crown of heaven, good man:

78 THE HOLLY AND THE IVY. (Irregular.)

Solo. In moderate time.

English Traditional Tune.

The hol-ly and the i - vy, When they are both full grown, Of all the trees that are in the wood, The hol - ly bears the crown:

CHORUS.

The ri-sing of the sun And the run-ning of the deer, The

(*Small notes, Organ.*)

88

play-ing of the mer-ry or-gan, Sweet sing-ing in the choir.

Nativity, Lent, Autumn.   *Old Carol.*

THE holly and the ivy,
    When they are both full grown,
Of all the trees that are in the wood,
The holly bears the crown:

The rising of the sun
And the running of the deer,
The playing of the merry organ,
Sweet singing in the choir.

2 The holly bears a blossom,
    As white as the lily flower,
And Mary bore sweet Jesus Christ,
To be our sweet Saviour:

3 The holly bears a berry,
    As red as any blood,
And Mary bore sweet Jesus Christ
To do poor sinners good:

4 The holly bears a prickle,
    As sharp as any thorn,
And Mary bore sweet Jesus Christ
On Christmas day in the morn:

5 The holly bears a bark,
    As bitter as any gall,
And Mary bore sweet Jesus Christ
For to redeem us all:

6. The holly and the ivy,
    When they are both full grown,
Of all the trees that are in the wood,
The holly bears the crown:

79° ESTAINES PARVA. (76.76.76. Irregular.)

In moderate time. Unison.

IMOGEN HOLST.

BERWICK STREET. (76.76.76. Irregular.)

In moderate time. Unison.

MARTIN SHAW.

Christina G. Rossetti, 1830–94.

THE Shepherds had an Angel,
  The Wise Men had a star;
But what have I, a little child,
  To guide me home from far,
Where glad stars sing together
  And singing angels are?

2 Lord Jesus is my guardian,
  So I can nothing lack:
The lambs lie in his bosom,
  Along life's dangerous track;
The wilful lambs that go astray
  He bleeding fetches back.

3 Lord Jesus is my guiding star,
  My beacon-light in heaven;
He leads me step by step along
  The path of life uneven;
He, true light, leads me to that land
  Whose day shall be as seven.

4 Those Shepherds through the lonely night
  Sat watching by their sheep,
Until they saw the heavenly host
  Who neither tire nor sleep,
All singing 'Glory, glory'
  In festival they keep.

5. Christ watches me, his little lamb,
  Cares for me day and night,
That I may be his own in heaven:
  So angels clad in white
Shall sing their 'Glory, glory'
  For my sake in the height.

80° GOSTERWOOD. (76. 76. D.)

In moderate time. English Traditional Melody.

Anon.

THE wise may bring their learning,
  The rich may bring their wealth,
And some may bring their greatness,
  And some bring strength and health:
We, too, would bring our treasures
  To offer to the King;
We have no wealth or learning—
  What shall we children bring?

2. We'll bring the many duties
    We have to do each day;
  We'll try our best to please him,
    At home, at school, at play:
  And better are these treasures
    To offer to our King
  Than richest gifts without them;
    Yet these a child may bring.

92

81° DANIEL. (L.M.)

In moderate time.

Irish Traditional Melody.

J. M. C. Crum.

TO God who makes all lovely things
  How happy must our praises be,
Each day a new surprise he brings
  To make us glad his world to see.

2 How plentiful must be the mines
    From which he gives his gold away;
  In March he gives us celandines,
    He gives us buttercups in May.

3 He grows the wheat and never stops;
    There's none can count the blades of green;
  And up among the elm-tree tops
    As many thousand leaves are seen.

4 And when the wheat is bound in sheaves
    He sends his wind among the trees,
  And down come all the merry leaves
    In yellow-twinkling companies.

5 On winter nights his quiet flakes
    Come falling, falling all the night,
  And when the world next morning wakes
    It finds itself all shining white.

6 He makes the sea that shines afar
    With waves that dance unceasingly;
  And every single little star
    That twinkles in the evening sky.

7. He made the people that I meet,
    The many people, great and small,
  In home and school, and down the street,
    And he made me to love them all.

82 CRADLE SONG. (11 11. 11 11.)

In moderate time.

WILLIAM JAMES KIRKPATRICK, 1838–1921.

(*By permission of Hope Publishing Company.*)

The Kingdom of Heaven.

N. B. L.

TO Jesus, our hero, our teacher, and friend!
  Who raises the fallen, the broken to mend:
We struggle and quarrel, but he brings release
And shows us the way to his wisdom and peace.

2 His Kingdom is coming, God's will shall be done,
  And kindness, and justice, and peace shall be won;
  Like the angels in heaven, his knights shall obey,
  Till sickness, and want, and disputes pass away.

3. God's name shall be hallowed, his love understood—
  The Father of all men, the wise and the good:
  The pagans shall see him in truth as he is,
  And the heart of the world shall for ever be his!

(*A pagan is a person who is not a Christian, whether in
Europe, Asia, Africa, America, or Australasia.*)

83 EPSOM. (C.M.)

In moderate time.

Melody in
Arnold's *Complete Psalter*, 1756.

William Blake, 1757–1827.

TO Mercy, Pity, Peace, and Love,
  All pray in their distress,
And to these virtues of delight
  Return their thankfulness.

2 For Mercy, Pity, Peace, and Love,
  Is God our Father dear;
And Mercy, Pity, Peace, and Love,
  Is Man, his child and care.

3 For Mercy has a human heart,
  Pity, a human face;
And Love, the human form divine,
  And Peace, the human dress.

4 Then every man, of every clime,
  That prays in his distress,
Prays to the human form divine:
  Love, Mercy, Pity, Peace.

5.*And all must love the human form,
  In heathen, Turk, or Jew;
Where Mercy, Love, and Pity dwell,
  There God is dwelling too.

84 EIA. (76.76.46.)

Moderately slow.   Old German Tune, 1638.

Eia.   *P. D. from the German.*

TO us in Bethlem city
  Was born a little son;
In him all gentle graces
  Were gathered into one,
    Eia, Eia,
  Were gathered into one.

2 And all our love and fortune
  Lie in his mighty hands;
Our sorrows, joys, and failures,
  He sees and understands,
    Eia, Eia,
  He sees and understands.

3 O Shepherd ever near us,
  We'll go where thou dost lead;
No matter where the pasture,
  With thee at hand to feed,
    Eia, Eia,
  With thee at hand to feed.

4. No grief shall part us from thee,
  However sharp the edge:
We'll serve, and do thy bidding—
  O take our hearts in pledge!
    Eia, Eia,
  Take thou our hearts in pledge!

(*For information about this and other Carols see the* Oxford Book of Carols.)

85° OMEGA AND ALPHA. (76.77.)

Moderately fast.
Full (Voices in Unison).

Arr. GEOFFREY SHAW.

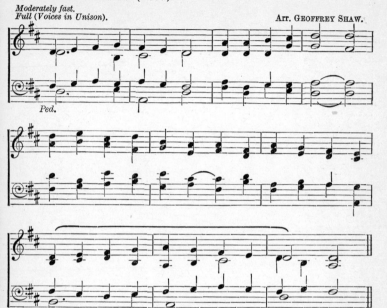

(A varied accompaniment for each verse will be found in the Oxford Carol Book, No. 92.)

15th-century Carol. Tr. P. D.

UNTO us a boy is born!
　　King of all creation,
Came he to a world forlorn,
　　The Lord of every nation.

2 Cradled in a stall was he
　　With sleepy cows and asses;
But the very beasts could see
　　That he all men surpasses.

3 Herod then with fear was filled:
　　'A prince', he said, 'in Jewry!'
All the little boys he killed
　　At Bethlem in his fury.

4 Now may Mary's son, who came
　　So long ago to love us,
Lead us all with hearts aflame
　　Unto the joys above us.

5. Omega and Alpha he!
　　Let the organ thunder,
While the choir with peals of glee
　　Doth rend the air asunder.

86° PUER NOBIS NASCITUR. (L.M.)

Composed or adapted by
M. PRAETORIUS, 1571–1621.

Moderately fast.

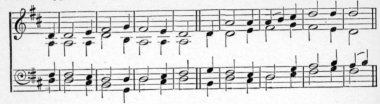

Mrs. C. F. Alexander, 1823–95.

WE are but little children weak,
  Nor born in any high estate;
What can we do for Jesus' sake,
  Who is so high and good and
    great?

2*We know the Holy Innocents
  Laid down for him their infant
    life,
And Martyrs brave and patient
    Saints
  Have stood for him in fire and
    strife.

3*We wear the cross they wore of old,
  Our lips have learned like vows to
    make;
We need not die, we cannot fight,—
  What may we do for Jesus' sake?

4 O, day by day, each Christian child
  Has much to do, without, with-
    in,—
A life to live for Jesus' sake,
  A constant war to wage with sin.

Part 2.

5 When deep within our swelling
    hearts
  The thoughts of pride and anger
    rise,
When bitter words are on our
    tongues,
  And tears of passion in our eyes,

6 Then we may stay the angry blow,
  Then we may check the hasty
    word,
Give gentle answers back again,
  And fight a battle for our Lord.

7 With smiles of peace and looks of
    love
  Light in our dwellings we may
    make,
Bid kind good-humour brighten
    there,
  And still do all for Jesus' sake.

8. There's not a child so small and weak
  But has his little cross to take,
His little work of love and praise
  That he may do for Jesus' sake!

87 ST. MARGARET. (88. 88. 44. 8.)

In moderate time.

G. W. BRIGGS.

(Copyright, 1929, by Oxford University Press.)

School.   *S. W. Meyer.*

WE build our school on thee, O
Lord;
  To thee we bring our common
    need,
The loving heart, the helpful word,
  The tender thought, the kindly
    deed:
    With these we pray
    Thy Spirit may
Enrich and bless our school alway.

2 We work together in thy sight,
  We live together in thy love;
Guide thou our faltering steps
    aright,
  And lift our thoughts to Heaven
    above:
    Dear Lord, we pray
    Thy Spirit may
Be present in our school alway.

3 Hold thou each hand to keep it just;
  Touch thou our lips, and make
    them pure;
If thou art with us, Lord, we must
  Be faithful friends and comrades
    sure:
    Dear Lord, we pray
    Thy Spirit may
Be present in our school alway.

4. We change, but thou art still the
    same—
  The same good Master, Teacher,
    Friend;
We change; but, Lord, we bear thy
    name,
  To journey with it to the end:
    And so we pray
    Thy Spirit may
Be present in our school alway.

88°   BIRTHDAY.   (12 12, 8 10.)

MARTIN SHAW.

In moderate time.

(*Copyright, 1915, by J. Curwen & Sons, Ltd.*)

Birthdays.

P. D.

WE wish you many happy returns of the day!
    We hope you may be healthy and strong all the way:
Strong to do right, slow to do wrong,
And thoughtful for others all the day long.

89° RESERVOIR. (C.M.)

Not too fast.

English Traditional Melody.

The Ships.

M. M. Penstone, 1859–1910.

WHEN lamps are lighted in the town,
　　The boats sail out to sea;
The fishers watch when night comes down,
　　They work for you and me.

2 We little children go to rest;
　　Before we sleep, we pray
　That God will bless the fishermen
　　And bring them back at day.

3 The boats come in at early dawn,
　　When children wake in bed,
　Upon the beach the boats are drawn,
　　And all the nets are spread.

4. God hath watched o'er the fishermen
　　Far on the deep dark sea,
　And brought them safely home again,
　　Where they are glad to be.

90   MAROWN. (76. 76. D.)

In moderate time.

Manx Traditional Tune.

Carol of the Kingdom.   *Steuart Wilson.*

WHEN Jesus was a baby
    And born of mortal men,
The first who asked to see him
    Came straight from their sheep-pen:
So let each one remember,
    When he his offering brings,
That Jesus loved the Shepherds
    As well as the three Kings.

2 When Jesus was a carpenter,
    He held the saw and adze,
And learned a trade to follow
    Like other simple lads:
So let us not be shamèd
    Of honest work and sweat,
Remembering that a better brow
    Than ours was often wet.

3 When Jesus was a-dying
    Upon the cruel tree,
Two thieves upon each hand of him
    He had for company:
So look not upon any man
    With vain or scornful eyes,
For one poor thief was called by him
    To dwell in Paradise.

4. Now Jesus has gone up on high,
    And truth and justice reign.
Let tenderness and kindliness
    Dwell in the hearts of men:
So, when we have to leave this earth,
    If only we can know
We leave it better than we found,
    We shall be glad to go.

91° GAMBLE. (65. 65. D.)

In moderate time. From an English Popular Melody.

(Copyright, 1929, by Oxford University Press)

Nativity. *William Canton, 1845–1926.*

WHEN the herds were watching
   In the midnight chill
Came a spotless lambkin
   From the heavenly hill.

2 Snow was on the mountains,
   And the wind was cold,
When from God's own garden
   Dropped a rose of gold.

3 When 'twas bitter winter,
   Homeless and forlorn
In a star-lit stable
   Christ the Babe was born.

4. Welcome, heavenly lambkin;
   Welcome, golden rose;
Alleluya, Baby
   In the swaddling clothes!

92° FAIRLIGHT. (55. 86. D.)

At a gentle pace. GEOFFREY SHAW.

Who has seen the wind? Nei-ther you nor I; . . . But

(Copyright, 1929, by Oxford University Press.)

104

GENERAL

when the trees bow down their heads, The wind is pass-ing

by. . . . The wind is pass-ing by. . . .

rit. . . . .

A tempo.

Who has seen the wind? Nei-ther I nor you; . . . But

when the leaves hang trem-bling, . . . The wind is pass-ing

through. The wind is pass-ing through. . . . . . .

rit.   *p*

The Unseen.   *Christina G. Rossetti (1830–94).*

105

93° RESONET IN LAUDIBUS. (7 8. 7 11.—and Refrain 10 9. 8 4. 4 10.)

Moderately fast. Voices in Unison.   German Carol Melody, 14th century.

Who with-in that sta-ble cries, Gen - tle babe that in

man - ger lies? 'Tis the Lord, our heart re - plies. So

fol - low him, his bid - ding do for ev - er:

Then let us all re - joice and sing, Re - joice and sing, with

106

one ac-cord! We will praise our friend and king, The Christ, The Lord, Ev - er, ev - er, Je - sus, bea - con for our high en-dea - vour!

P. D.

2 Who is he, the man full-grown,
  Working on in the busy town?
   'Tis the Lord obscure, unknown.
  So follow him, his bidding do for
   ever:

3 Healing lame and blind and dumb,
  Herald now that the Kingdom's
   come?
   'Tis the Friend of every home.
  So follow him, his bidding do for
   ever:

4 Who is he whom crowds acclaim
  As he enters Jerusalem?
   'Tis the Lord of happy fame.
  So follow him, his bidding do for
   ever:

5 Taken in Gethsemane,
  Martyred on the forlorn cross-tree?
   He who died for you and me.
  So follow him, his bidding do for
   ever:

6 From the tomb triumphant now,
  Deathless splendour upon his brow?
   He to whom all creatures bow.
  So follow him, his bidding do for
   ever:

7. Passing still to every place,
  Radiant friend of the human race!
   'Tis the Lord, the fount of
   grace.
  So follow him, his bidding do for
   ever:

(*This may be sung as a solo, the chorus, or the first four lines of it, being sung by all.*)

107

PART III

SPECIAL HYMNS, ETC.

The People Oversea
Graces, &c.
Thanksgiving and Praise
The Song of the Creatures
Processional
Doxologies

94° MAGDALENA. (76. 76.)

German Traditional Melody
(16th cent. ?).

In moderate time.

Children's Oversea Hymn.

P. D.

REMEMBER all the people
  Who live in far-off lands
In strange and lovely cities,
  Who roam the desert sands,

2 Or farm the mountain pastures,
  Or till the endless plains
Where children splash in rice-fields
  And watch the camel-trains:

3 Some work in sultry forests
  Where apes swing to and fro,
Some fish in mighty rivers,
  Some hunt across the snow.

4 Remember all God's children,
  Who yet have never heard
The truth that comes from Jesus,
  The glory of his word.

5 God bless the men and women
  Who serve him oversea,
God raise up more to help them,
  And fill their hearts with glee,

6. Till all the distant people
  In every foreign place
Shall understand his Kingdom
  And come into his grace.

108

THE PEOPLE OVERSEA

MARATHON. (87. 87. D.)

Voices in Unison. In moderate march time.

R. VAUGHAN WILLIAMS.

Ser-vants of the great ad-ven-ture, Pa-triots of God's fa-ther-land,

con 8va.

Fired by one su - preme am - bi - tion, Rea - dy for the

call we stand. Cleanse our minds, thou Love all - rul - ing,

(Copyright, 1928, by R. Vaughan Williams.)

109

Steel our wills, un-bind our eyes That we see a-right thy King-dom; Make us dar-ing, free, ... and wise.

The Round World.   P. D.

2 Christ to us across the water
    Came of old from Palestine,
West and ever farther westward
    Came the eastern Light to shine;
Long and stubborn was the struggle
    Ere our fathers' hearts were won;
Often have we warped the message,
    Been as clouds before the sun.

3*But, for all our faults and failures,
    'Tis through Christ the West has
        grown;
And 'tis ours to give to others
    What we dare not keep alone.
Death will come and crumbling
        chaos,
    If we share not with the earth
That which tempers might with
        mercy,
    Gives to science human worth.

4*We have probed, and piled up know-
        ledge,
    Weighed the stars, and wrought
        our will,
Marshalled fire and harnessed light-
        ning,
    Made men gods for good or ill:
Only that which bred our greatness—
    Freedom, all the truth to find,
Love revealed in One Perfection—
    Is not fathomed by mankind.

5*Millions lie in crying darkness,
    Unredeemed, untamed, untaught,
Women prone in sealed oppression,
    Men like cattle sold and bought;
Millions grope through outworn
        systems;
    Many a cruel ancient faith
Binds the earth, and many a rebel
    Dooms the Christ again to death.

6*Yet men everywhere have found thee,
    Christ, the crown of every creed;
All the faiths and all the systems
    To thy revelation lead;
Thou dost guide our human groping,
    Who hast won the souls of men;
Thou wilt fill the world with splendour—
    In our hands the how and when.

7 Thou art building up a city,
    Pictured perfect in thy thought;
And from glimpses of that pattern
    All man's fairest things are wrought:
Thou dost call as fellow-workers
    Us, to serve thy great design:
Thou the Artist, thou the Maker,
    Dost to each his part assign.

8 All the world shall live in kindness,
    Hate and war shall pass away,
When men grow from out the blindness,
    Wake, and see the blaze of day:
Each but needs the truth to win him,
    Shape the beauty of his soul,
Strike the fire of love within him,
    Save from self and make him whole.

9. Praise God for the hidden leaven,
    For the depths yet unexplored;
Praise him for the Realm of Heaven—
    All ye peoples, praise the Lord!
Sing, the round world all together,
    With one mind and heart and mouth;
Glorify the Lord All-Father,
    East and West and North and South!

The simpler verses are left unstarred: the first two and last two only, or verses 2, 3, 8, and 9 can be sung. More may be wanted for a procession.

See also :

    16 Jesus shall reign
    68 Little drops of water
    82 To Jesus, our hero

96° PADDOCKS. (77. 77. 77.)

Simply, and not too fast.

GEOFFREY SHAW.

Here a lit-tle child I stand, Heav-ing up my ei - ther hand; Cold as pad-docks though they be, Here I lift them up to thee,

GRACES

For a ben - i - son to fall

On our meat and on us all. A - men.

Herrick's Grace.   *Robert Herrick, 1591–1674.*

HERE a little child I stand,
  Heaving up my either hand;
Cold as paddocks though they be,
Here I lift them up to thee,
For a benison to fall
On our meat and on us all.

(Paddocks are toads : a benison is a blessing.)

97° PACHELBEL. (88. 8 88.)

Rather slow.

? J. PACHELBEL, 1653–1706.

Our Fa - ther, for our dai - ly bread Ac - cept our praise and

hear our prayer. By thee all liv - ing souls are fed:

Thy boun - ty and thy lov - ing care

With all thy chil - dren let us share.

Grace before Meals.

G. W. Briggs.

See also 103, 105, and the Doxologies.

COLLECTION

(*Copyright*, 1915, by *J. Curwen & Sons, Ltd.*)

98°   OPPIDANS MEWS.   (6 5. 6 5.)

Brightly.   MARTIN SHAW.

1 Here we come with glad - ness, Gifts of
2 Small may be the offer - ing, But the
3. More and more for Je - sus May we

love to bring, Prais - ing him who
Lord will use Ev - 'ry gift we
glad - ly give; Giv - ing, giv - ing,

loves us— Christ our Sa - viour King.
bring him; None will he re - fuse.
giv - ing, Is the way to live.

Collection March.   *Julia H. Johnston.*

For the other Kindergarten hymns see note to No. 102.

99 ROYDEN. (66.446, and refrain.)

With breadth.

MARTIN SHAW.

O wel-come in our midst, Your life with us re - new! With all our heart, From ev -'ry part Our love we give to you: *Length to your days!*

GREETING

Strength to your ways! Bless-ings, bless-ings be up - on your head! head! . . . .

(Copyright U.S.A., 1929, by Martin Shaw.)

Song of Greeting.   **P. D.**

O WELCOME in our midst,
 Your life with us renew!
  With all our heart,
  From every part
 Our love we give to you:
  Length to your days!
  Strength to your ways!
  Blessings be upon your head!

2 May faith and love be yours,
  And laughter gem your way;
   And may you find
   Clouds silver-lined—
  And all your work as play:

3 From hurt of foe, or friend,
  From envy, faction, spite,
   May you be kept,
   And live adept
  At turning dark to light:

4.*May triumph crown your plans,
  And hope maintain your youth;
   In God's dear peace
   May you increase
  And find your goal in truth:

*Verse 1 for any new-comer at school. The whole (or three verses) for a new parson or teacher, or
at the beginning of term. Verses 2 and 3 (and 4) may be sung at the end of term, or as a farewell.
See also No. 87; and for the end of term Nos. 70, 101, 104 (Pt. 2), 106 (Pt. 1), 109.*

100   MONKLAND.   (7 7. 7 7.)

In moderate time.

Origin unknown,
'arranged by J. WILKES' (1861).

Ps. 136.

J. *Milton* ‡, 1608–74.

LET us, with a gladsome mind,
Praise the Lord, for he is kind:
For his mercies ay endure,
Ever faithful, ever sure.

2 Let us blaze his name abroad,
For of gods he is the God:

3 He with all-commanding might
Filled the new-made world with
light:

4 He the golden-tressèd sun
Caused all day his course to run:

5 The hornèd moon to shine by night,
'Mid her spangled sisters bright:

6 All things living he doth feed,
His full hand supplies their need:

7. Let us, with a gladsome mind,
Praise the Lord, for he is kind :

A - men.

101   NUN DANKET.   (6 7. 6 7. 6 6. 6 6.)

Very slow and majestic.

Present form of melody by
J. CRÜGER, 1598–1662.

Org.

THANKSGIVING AND PRAISE

Thanksgiving.　　　　　*M. Rinkart, 1586–1649. Tr. C. Winkworth.*

Nun danket alle Gott.

Now thank we all our God,
　With heart and hands and voices,
Who wondrous things hath done,
In whom his world rejoices;
　Who from our mother's arms
　　Hath blessed us on our way
With countless gifts of love,
　　And still is ours to-day.

2　　O may this bounteous God
Through all our life be near us,
　With ever joyful hearts
And blessèd peace to cheer us;
　And keep us in his grace,
　　And guide us when perplexed,
　And free us from all ills
　　In this world and the next.

3.　　All praise and thanks to God
The Father now be given,
　The Son, and him who reigns
With them in highest heaven,
　The one eternal God,
　　Whom earth and heaven adore;
For thus it was, is now,
　　And shall be evermore.

A - men.

119

(Copyright, 1915, by J. Curwen & Sons, Ltd.)

102° MANOR STREET. (10. 6 D.)

Allegro. MARTIN SHAW.

Praise him, praise him, all ye lit-tle chil-dren! He is love, he is love. Praise him, praise him, all ye lit-tle chil-dren! He is love, he is love.

Anon.

P RAISE him, praise him, all ye little children!
He is love, he is love.

2 Thank him, thank him, all ye little children!
He is love, he is love.

3 Love him, love him, all ye little children!
He is love, he is love.

4. Crown him, crown him, all ye little children!
He is love, he is love.

Both lines of each verse are repeated. (For the other Kindergarten hymns see No. 98, and the Sunday Kindergarten Service in *Short Services*, bound up with this book. The music of the Sunday Kindergarten is in *Song Time*, Curwen & Sons.)

THANKSGIVING AND PRAISE

103° BATTISHILL. (77.77.)

In moderate time.

JONATHAN BATTISHILL, 1738–1801.

E. Rutter Leatham.

THANK you! for the world so sweet,
Thank you! for the food we eat,
Thank you! for the birds that sing,
Thank you! God, for everything.

104 AUSTRIAN HYMN. (87. 87. D.)

Moderately slow.

F. J. HAYDN, 1732–1809.

Ps. 148.

Foundling Hospital Coll. (1796).

PRAISE the Lord! ye heavens, adore him;
  Praise him, Angels, in the height;
Sun and moon, rejoice before him,
  Praise him, all ye stars and light:
Praise the Lord! for he hath spoken,
  Worlds his mighty voice obeyed;
Laws, which never shall be broken,
  For their guidance hath he made.

THANKSGIVING AND PRAISE

2 Praise the Lord! for he is glorious;
　　Never shall his promise fail;
　God hath made his Saints victorious,
　　Sin and death shall not prevail.
　Praise the God of our salvation;
　　Hosts on high, his power proclaim;
　Heaven and earth, and all creation,
　　Laud and magnify his name!

Part 2.　　　　　　*E. Osler*, 1798–1863.

3. Worship, honour, glory, blessing,
　　Lord, we offer to thy name;
　Young and old, thy praise expressing,
　　Join their Saviour to proclaim.
　As the Saints in heaven adore thee,
　　We would bow before thy throne;
　As thine Angels serve before thee,
　　So on earth thy will be done.

A - men.

105°　MAGDALENA. (7 6. 7 6.)

German Traditional Melody
(16th cent.?).

In moderate time.

WE thank thee, loving Father,
　　For all thy tender care,
For food and clothes and shelter
　And all the world so fair.

123

106 ALL CREATURES.

In the time of slow reading.

Set to a Parisian Tone and an original
tune by MARTIN SHAW.

1 O most high, almighty, good Lord God: praise, glory, and honour, to thee belong all bless-ing.

2 Prais-ed be my Lord God, with all his crea-tures: and specially our brother the Sun, who brings us the Day and who brings us the Light.

3 Fair is he, and shining with a ve-ry great splen-dour: O Lord, he signifies to us thee.

(Copyright U.S.A., 1926, by Martin Shaw.)

THE SONG OF THE CREATURES

4 Prais - ed   be my Lord for our   sis - ter the Moon:
5 Prais - ed   be my Lord for our   bro - ther the Wind:

and for the Stars, the which he has set clear and love - ly in hea - ven.
and for Air and Cloud, calms, and all weather by the which thou upholdest in life all crea - tures.

6 Praisèd be my Lord for our   sis - ter   Wa - ter:

who is very serviceable unto us, and humble and pre-cious and clean.

f

7 Prais-ed be my Lord for our brother Fire, through whom thou givest us light in the dark-ness:

8 Prais-ed be my Lord for our mother the Earth, the which doth sustain us and keep us:

and he is bright and pleasant and very migh-ty and strong.
and bringeth forth divers fruits, and flowers of many col-ours, and grass.

v. 8.

THE SONG OF THE CREATURES

Part II.

*9 Praisèd be my Lord
for all those who
pardon one another
for his love's sake:
and who endure
weakness and
tri-bu-la-tion,

*10 Bless-ed are they who
peaceably
shall en-dure:
for thou, O most
Highest, shalt
give them a crown.

*11 Praisèd be my Lord for our sister the death of the bo-dy:

Blessed are they who are found walking by thy most ho - ly will.

Doxology to either part.

12. Praise ye and bless ye the Lord and give thanks un - to him:

and serve him with great hu - mi - li - ty. *Al - le - lu - ya, Al - le - lu - ya!*

St. Francis of Assisi (Tr. Matthew Arnold).

St. Francis was born about 1182. He made Part I with the Doxology first. In 1226 he added verses 9 and 10, and later in that year, a little while before he died, he added verse 11, which is shortened in Arnold's translation, and here.

PART III

107° WULFRUN. (888.)

In moderate time.

G. W. BRIGGS.

(Copyright, 1929, by Oxford University Press.)

George Herbert, 1593–1632.

ENRICH, Lord, heart, mouth, hands in me,
  With faith, with hope, with charity:
That I may run, rise, rest with thee.

108° MADDERMARKET. (11. 11. 11. and refrain.)

In moderate time. Parts 1, 2, 4, and Conclusion. MARTIN SHAW.

(*Copyright, 1929, by Oxford University Press.*)

Onward ever. P. D.

Part 1.

O FATHER above us, our father in might,
All live by thy love, as the flowers in the light;
Our father and mother and maker art thou:
Forward !
Forward ever, forward now !

2 In thee move the infinite stars on their rounds,
The planets, the sun, and the moon in their bounds,
As they kindle and glitter and sparkle and glow:
Onward !
Onward ever, onward go !

3 The flowers in our gardens of every gay hue,
The meadows and sky-world, the green and the blue,
All show us thy mind, for thou makest them so:

4 The plants are all breathing, the stones are alive,
   The atoms are busy, like bees in a hive,
     And forces invisible spin to and fro:

5 And thou art the maker of beautiful things,
   Like roses and daisies and butterflies' wings,
     And mountains and forests, and water and snow:

B.

6 The cloud-mists rise up from the sea, by thy hand,
   And bring life to all, as they water the land,
     Then back to the ocean as rivers they flow:

7 All creatures are thine in the world and beyond,
   The bee in the pollen, the fish in the pond,
     The fox in his burrow, the bird on the bough:

8 The lambs and the calves and the foals that are born,
   The beans and potatoes, the roots and the corn,
     The apple and cherry trees, row after row:

9 And thine are the herds of the cattle and sheep,
   And lions, and monsters who surge in the deep,
     And sea-birds who float on the winds as they blow:

C.

10 And thine are the men in the mills and the mines,
   The factories, offices, stations, and lines,
     The airplanes and steamers that pass to and fro:

11 The smith at his anvil, the cook by her fire,
   The builders, the painters, the men in the choir,
     The diggers and weavers and women who sew:

12 And children who sing by the sea on the sand,
   Who sing in their schools, and who dance on the land,
     And toss up the hay that the labourers mow:

Part 2.

13 We thank thee for happiness, healthiness, love,
   For thoughts and for whispers that come from above,
     For good things we think of and good things we do:

14 We thank thee for games, and for friendship and fun,
   And the strength in our limbs when we caper and run,
     And all that is good and delightful and true:

15 Yes, we praise thee for goodness and beauty and truth;
   And we pray that we learn in the days of our youth
     To love all the gifts that from thee overflow:

16 *** So we lift up our hands and we sing out thy praise,
   While the banners go forward, and lights are ablaze,
     And the organ peals out, and the trumpeters blow:

ALDEBY. (11. 11. 11. and refrain.)

In moderate time.   Part 3.   MARTIN SHAW.

(*Copyright, 1929, by Oxford University Press.*)

ONWARD EVER

Part 3.

17 As we forgive others, forgive us our debts,
   Preserve us from evil,—from anger and threats,
      And all that is mean and deceitful and low:

18 From cruelty, slander, and keeping things back,
   From white lies and grey lies and lies that are black,
      And every temptation to draw the long bow:

19 And keep us from making a fuss of our woes,
   From sulks and from fretfulness, rudeness and blows;
      To peace make us quick, and to quarrelling slow:

20 O give us the grace not to wrangle or fight,
   And give us the wisdom to know what is right,
      And when to say Yes, and the way to say No:

21 So, active and healthy in body and mind,
   And nice to each other, unselfish and kind,
      And ever more faithful to thee we would grow:

22 And as we grow older, Lord, help us to learn,
   That wisdom and truth we may always discern,
      And follow with patience the way thou wilt show:

MADDERMARKET. (11. 11. 11. and refrain.)

In moderate time. MARTIN SHAW.

(*Copyright, 1929, by Oxford University Press.*)

Part 4.

23 We pray for our fathers and mothers, who give
   Our food and our clothes and the homes where we live:
   O teach us to pay them the debt that we owe:

24 On brothers and sisters, relations and friends,
   Each helper and teacher, and each one who spends
   Her time on the children, thy blessing bestow:

ONWARD EVER

25 And we pray for our rulers in Church and in State,
   For all, for the wise and the learned and great,
      For neighbour and stranger, for friend and for foe:

26 O bless all the people in lands overseas,
   Like Africans, Indians, Japs, and Chinese,
      And bring all the nations thy Gospel to know:

27 And show us thy light when our notions are wrong,
   Make the ill to be well, and the weak to be strong,
      And all that is evil and false overthrow ⚡

Conclusion.

28 We praise thee, O Father of infinite might,
   We thank thee for life and for love and for light,
      We pray thee thy treasure on all to bestow:

29 Our Father thou art whom all creatures obey,
   Thy Son to all people on earth shows the way,
      Thy Spirit gives light to our minds here below:

30. O God in whose working we live and we move,
    Through Jesus we know that thy nature is love:
       O teach us, O lead us, the way we should go—
          Onward,
          Onward bravely, here below !

A - men.

This may be sung as one long processional hymn, such as may be needed on massed festivals: or
some only of the Parts may be sung, ending with the Conclusion. Each or any Part may have the
star verse ✱✱ 16 (with action) sung at the end (there ought to be trumpeters). Short hymns can be
made of any section, (A), B, or C, or of any Part, with or without the Conclusion, which last may also
be sung alone as a Doxology.

(Even those who cannot read can still sing the refrain to each verse, 'Onward ever, onward go,'
while others sing the verses.)

109 ST. AUSTIN. (C.M.)   Parts 1, 2, and 4.

In moderate time.

English Traditional Melody.

FARNHAM. (C.M.)   Part 3.
In moderate time.

From an English Traditional Melody.

The Psalm of Sion.

W. Prid, 1585, and 'F.B.P.', c. 1585.

O MOTHER dear, Jerusalem,
  The throne of God on high,
O sacred city, queen, and wife
  Of Christ eternally!

2 O happy harbour of the Saints!
  O sweet and pleasant soil!
In thee no sorrow may be found,
  No grief, no care, no toil.

3 In thee no sickness may be seen,
  No hurt, no ache, no sore;

In thee there is no dread of death,
  But life for evermore.

4 No dampish mist is seen in thee,
  No cold nor darksome night;
There every soul shines as the sun;
  There God himself gives light.

5 There lust and lucre cannot dwell;
  There envy bears no sway;
There is no hunger, heat, nor cold,
  But pleasure every way.

136

THE PSALM OF SION

Part 2.

6 Jerusalem, Jerusalem,
   God grant I once may see
Thy endless joys, and of the same
   Partaker ay may be!

7 Thy walls are made of precious
      stones,
   Thy bulwarks diamonds square;
Thy gates are of right orient pearl,
   Exceeding rich and rare;

8 Thy turrets and thy pinnacles
   With carbuncles do shine;
Thy very streets are paved with
      gold,
   Surpassing clear and fine;

9 Thy houses are of ivory,
   Thy windows crystal clear;
Thy tiles are made of beaten gold—
   O God that I were there!

10 Within thy gates no thing doth
      come
   That is not passing clean,
No spider's web, no dirt, no dust,
   No filth may there be seen.

Part 3.

11 Thy Saints are crowned with glory
      great;
   They see God face to face;
They triumph still, they still rejoice:
   Most happy is their case.

12 And there they live in such delight,
   Such pleasure and such play,
As that to them a thousand years
   Doth seem as yesterday.

13 Thy vineyards and thy orchards are
   Most beautiful and fair,
Full furnishèd with trees and fruits,
   Most wonderful and rare;

14 Thy gardens and thy gallant walks
   Continually are green;
There grow such sweet and pleasant
      flowers
   As nowhere else are seen.

15 There's nectar and ambrosia made,
   There's musk and civet sweet;
There many a fair and dainty drug
   Is trodden under feet.

16 There cinnamon, there sugar grows,
   There nard and balm abound;
What tongue can tell, or heart con-
      ceive,
   The joys that there are found!

Part 4.

17 Quite through the streets with
      silver sound
   The flood of life doth flow,
Upon whose banks on every side
   The wood of life doth grow.

18 There trees for evermore bear fruit,
   And evermore do spring;
There evermore the Angels sit,
   And evermore do sing;

19 O then thrice happy, should my
      state
   In happiness remain,
If I might once thy glorious seat
   And princely place attain,

20 And view thy gallant gates, thy
      walls,
   Thy streets and dwellings wide,
Thy noble troop of citizens
   And mighty King beside.

21 He is the King of kings, beset
   Amidst his servants right;
And they, his happy household all,
   Do serve him day and night.

22. O mother dear, Jerusalem,
      The comfort of us all,
   How sweet thou art and delicate;
      No thing shall thee befall!

See also: 17 A child this day is born
            18 God rest you merry
            21 O come, all ye faithful
            22 The first Nowell
            95 Servants of the great adventure

(*It is a good plan to end a Procession with a Doxology—the number
being first announced—and the Blessing.*)

110° WAREHAM. (L.M.)

Very slow and dignified.

W. KNAPP, 1698 (?)–1768.

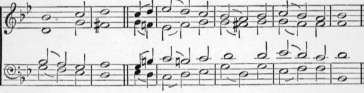

Ps. 117.

I. Watts, 1674–1748.

FROM all that dwell below the skies
  Let the Creator's praise arise:
Let the Redeemer's name be sung
Through every land by every tongue.

2. Eternal are thy mercies, Lord,
  Eternal truth attends thy word:
Thy praise shall sound from shore to shore,
Till suns shall rise and set no more.

A - men.

111   MIT FREUDEN ZART.   (87. 87. 887.)

In moderate time.   Unison.   Hymn Melody of the Bohemian Brethren.

(By permission of Messrs. N. Simrock, and Alfred Lengnick & Co., Ltd., from Riemann's 'Das Deutsche Geistliche Lied'.)

M. F. Bell.

O DEAREST Lord, by all adored,
    Our trespasses confessing,
To thee this day thy children pray,
    The holy Faith professing !
Accept, O King, the gifts we bring,
Our songs of praise, the prayers we raise ;
And grant us, Lord, thy blessing.

A - men.

112° MARTYRDOM. (C.M.)

Slow.

Smith's *Sacred Music*, 1825.
Possibly an Old Scottish Melody.

C.M.

Old Psalter.

T O Father, Son, and Holy Ghost,
   The God whom we adore,
Be glory, as it was, is now,
   And shall be evermore.

A - men.

113° ST. THOMAS. (S.M.)

In moderate time.

Williams' Psalmody, 1770.

S.M.   *P.D.*

TO thee who makest all,
    High praise and glory be,
Who goodness, truth, and beauty art
    Through all eternity.

A - men.

See also:
    5, v. 2 North and south
    7, v. 4 Praise God, from whom all blessings flow (L.M.)
    10, v. 8 Glory to the Father
    21, v. 6 Sing, choirs of angels
    24, v. 6 All glory be to God on high
    26, vv. 1, 2 All glory, laud, and honour
    37, v. 5 To Father, Son, and Holy Ghost (L.M.)
    100, v. 1 Let us, with a gladsome mind
    101, v. 3 All praise and thanks to God
    104, v. 1 Praise the Lord! ye heavens, adore him
    104, v. 3 Worship, honour, glory, blessing
    108, vv. 28–30 We praise thee, O Father of infinite might

METRICAL INDEX OF TUNES

77. 77. 77.
Paddocks, 96.
Voller Wunder, 6.

78. 7 11. (*and refrain*).
Resonet in laudibus, 93.

83. 83. 77. 87.
Springtime, 12.

85. 83.
Westridge, 66.

86. 86. 8. (*and refrain*).
Joys seven, 77.

86. 86. 86. (*and refrain*).
God rest you merry, 18.

87. 87.
Shipston, 8.

87. 87. D.
Austrian Hymn, 104.
Marathon, 95.
Pleading Saviour, 57.

87. 877.
Il buon pastor, 70.

87. 87. 77.
Irby, 74.

87. 87. 887.
Mit freuden zart, 111.
Trefaenan, 42.

888.
Wulfrun, 107.

88. 87.
Come, faithful people, 27.
Quem pastores lauda-
vere, 65.

88. (*with refrain*).
I saw three ships, 20.

88. 88. 44. 8.
St. Margaret, 87.

88. 888.
Pachelbel, 97.

10 2. 10 2. 886.
The Birds, 47.

10 4. 66. 66. 10 4.
High Road, 67.

10 6. 10 6.
Manor Street, 102.

10. 10.
A little child, 19.
Garden, 2.

11. 11. 11. 2. 7.
Aldeby, 108.
Maddermarket, 108.

11 11. 11 11.
Cradle Song, 82.

11 11. 12 11.
Monks Gate, 56.

12 12. 8 10.
Birthday, 88.

Irregular.
Adeste fideles, 21.
All creatures, 106.
Constantia, 50.
David, 50.
East Horndon, 60.
I saw three ships, 20.
Tavistock, 9.
The First Nowell, 22.
The Holly and the Ivy, 78.

ALPHABETICAL INDEX OF TUNES

INDEX OF COMPOSERS, ARRANGERS, AND SOURCES OF MELODIES

INDEX OF AUTHORS, ETC.

(The numbers in brackets refer to translations)

GENERAL INDEX

No.	FIRST LINE	METRE	NAME OF TUNE
36	A brighter dawn is breaking	7 7.7 7.	Nun lasst uns Gott dem Herren.
17	A child this day is born	S.M. and refrain	Sandys.
19	A little child on the earth has been born	Irregular	A little child.
26	All glory, laud, and honour	7 6.7 6. D.	St. Theodulph (Valet will ich dir geben).
37	All people that on earth do dwell	L.M.	Old Hundredth.
38	All things bright and beautiful	7 6.7 6. D. and refrain	Royal Oak.
39	All things which live below the sky	C.M.	Evan.
33	Around the throne of God a band	L.M.	Solothurn.
40	As Joseph was a-walking	7 6.7 6.	Cherry.
41	Can I see another's woe	7 7.7 7.	Galliard.
42	Can you count the stars that brightly	8 7.8 7.8 8 7.	Trefaenan.
27	Come, faithful people, come away	8 8.8 7.	Come, faithful people.
31	Come, let us join our cheerful songs	C.M.	Cheerful.
43	Day by day	3 8.6 5.6 3.	Fairfield.
3	Dear Father, keep me through this day	C.M.	St. Botolph.
44	Do no sinful action	6 5.6 5.	Newland.
107	Enrich, Lord, heart, mouth, hands in me	8 8 8.	Wulfrun.
45	Every morning the red sun	7 5.7 5.7 7.	Langdale.
46	Everything changes	5 5.6 5.8 7. 8 7.	Gun Hill.
14	Fair waved the golden corn	S.M.	Selma.
4	Father, we thank thee for the night	L.M.	Morning Hymn.
34	For all thy Saints, O Lord	S.M.	Mount Ephraim.
25	Forty days and forty nights	7 7.7 7.	Aus der Tiefe.
110	From all that dwell below the skies	L.M.	Wareham.
47	From out of a wood did a cuckoo fly	10 2.10 2. 8 8 6.	The Birds.

148

GENERAL INDEX

No.	First Line	Metre	Name of Tune
48	Gentle Jesus, meek and mild	7 7.7 7.	Gentle Jesus.
49	Glad that I live am I	6 5. 6 5. Irregular	Water-End.
7	Glory to thee, my God, this night	L.M.	Tallis' Canon.
50	God be in my head	Irregular Irregular	1. Constantia. 2. David.
51	God is love, his the care	6 6 6.6 6.5 5. 3 9.	Theodoric.
52	God made little Robin	6 5.6 5.	Glenfinlas.
53	God my Father, loving me	7 7.7 7.	St. Joan.
18	God rest you merry, Gentlemen	8 6.8 6.8 6. and refrain	God rest you merry.
54	God who made the earth	5 6.6 4.	Hermitage.
55	God whose name is Love	5 5.5 5.	Haslemere.
12	Hark, a hundred notes are swelling	8 3.8 3.7 7. 8 7.	Springtime.
56	He who would valiant be	11 11.12 11.	Monks Gate.
57	Heavenly Father, send thy blessing	8 7.8 7. D.	Pleading Saviour.
96	Here a little child I stand	7 7.7 7.7 7.	Paddocks.
98	Here we come with gladness	6 5.6 5.	Oppidans Mews.
58	How far is it to Bethlehem	7 4.7 4. Irregular	Stowey.
59	I love God's tiny creatures	7 6.7 6. D.	Ellacombe.
20	I saw three ships come sailing in	Irregular	I saw three ships.
60	I think, when I read that sweet story of old	Irregular	East Horndon.
61	In another land and time	7 7.7 7.	Peacefield.
62	In every town and village	7 4.7 4.10.6 6.	Bell Carol.
63	In our work, and in our play	7 7.7 7.	Lyne.
64	It is a thing most wonderful	L.M.	Herongate.
65	Jesu, good above all other	8 8.8 7.	Quem pastores laudavere.
8	Jesu, tender Shepherd, hear me	8 7.8 7.	Shipston.
30	Jesus Christ is risen to-day	7 4.7 4. D.	Easter Hymn.
66	Jesus, friend of little children	8 5.8 3.	Westridge.
16	Jesus shall reign where'er the sun	L.M.	Truro.
67	Let all the world in every corner sing	10 4.6 6.6 6. 10 4.	High Road.
100	Let us, with a gladsome mind	7 7.7 7.	Monkland.
68	Little drops of water	6 5.6 5.	Gott ein Vater.
69	Lord, I would own thy tender care	C.M.	Eardisley.
70	Lord of health, thou life within us	8 7.8 7 7.	Il buon pastor.
71	Loving Shepherd of thy sheep	7 7.7 7.	Innocents.

No.	First Line	Metre	Name of Tune
9	Matthew, Mark, and Luke, and John	Irregular	Tavistock.
101	Now thank we all our God	67.6 7.6 6.6 6.	Nun danket.
10	Now the day is over	6 5.6 5.	Eudoxia.
21	O come, all ye faithful	Irregular	Adeste fideles.
72	O dear and lovely Brother	7 6.7 6.	Hambridge.
111	O dearest Lord, by all adored	8 7.8 7.8 8 7.	Mit freuden zart.
108	O Father above us, our father in might	11.11.11.2.7. 11.11.11.2.7.	1. Maddermarket. 2. Aldeby.
32	O Holy Spirit, God	S.M.	St. Edmund.
106	O most high, almighty, good Lord God	Irregular	All creatures.
109	O mother dear, Jerusalem	C.M. C.M.	1. St. Austin. 2. Farnham.
73	O sweeter than the marriage-feast	C.M.	Harington (Retirement).
99	O welcome in our midst	6 6.4 4 6. and refrain	Royden.
74	Once in royal David's city	8 7.8 7.7 7.	Irby.
97	Our Father, for our daily bread	8 8.8 8 8.	Pachelbel.
102	Praise him, praise him, all ye little children	10 6.10 6.	Manor Street.
104	Praise the Lord! ye heavens, adore him	8 7.8 7. D.	Austrian Hymn.
94	Remember all the people	7 6.7 6.	Magdalena.
75	Saviour, teach me, day by day	7 7.7 7.	Boyce.
29	See him in raiment rent	6 4.6 3. D. 6 4.6 3. D.	1. Bridgwater. 2. Langport.
95	Servants of the great adventure	8 7.8 7. D.	Marathon.
76	Sing to the Lord the children's hymn	C.M.	St. Hugh.
1	So here hath been dawning	6 5.6 5. Irregular	Hardwick.
11	Sun of my soul, thou Saviour dear	L.M.	Birling.
103	Thank you! for the world so sweet	7 7.7 7.	Battishill.
77	The first good joy that Mary had	8 6.8 6. and refrain	Joys seven.
22	The first Nowell the angel did say	Irregular	The First Nowell.
78	The holly and the ivy	Irregular	The Holly and the Ivy.
79	The Shepherds had an Angel	7 6.7 6.7 6. 7 6.7 6.7 6.	1. Estaines Parva. 2. Berwick Street.
35	The Son of God goes forth to war	C.M.	St. Anne.

GENERAL INDEX

No.	First Line	Metre	Name of Tune
80	The wise may bring their learning	7 6.7 6. D.	Gosterwood.
13	The year's at the spring	5 5.4 5. D.	Bamberg.
28	There is a green hill far away	C.M.	Horsley.
6	Thou who once on mother's knee	7 7.7 7.7 7.	Voller Wunder.
5	Through the night thy Angels kept	7 7.7 7.	Horsham.
112	To Father, Son, and Holy Ghost	C.M.	Martyrdom.
81	To God who makes all lovely things	L.M.	Daniel.
82	To Jesus, our hero, our teacher, and friend	11 11.11 11.	Cradle Song.
83	To Mercy, Pity, Peace, and Love	C.M.	Epsom.
113	To thee who makest all	S.M.	St. Thomas.
84	To us in Bethlem city	7 6.7 6.4 6.	Eia.
85	Unto us a boy is born	7 6.7 7.	Omega and Alpha.
86	We are but little children weak	L.M.	Puer nobis nascitur.
87	We build our school on thee, O Lord	8 8.8 8.4 4.8.	St. Margaret.
105	We thank thee, loving Father	7 6.7 6.	Magdalena.
88	We wish you many happy returns of the day	12 12.8 10.	Birthday.
23	When Christ was born in Bethlehem	C.M.	Rodwell.
90	When Jesus was a baby	7 6.7 6. D.	Marown.
89	When lamps are lighted in the town	C.M.	Reservoir.
91	When the herds were watching	6 5.6 5. D.	Gamble.
2	When virgin morn doth call thee to arise	10.10.	Garden.
24	While shepherds watched their flocks by night	C.M.	Winchester Old.
92	Who has seen the wind?	5 5.8 6. D.	Fairlight.
93	Who within that stable cries	7 8.7 11. and refrain	Resonet in laudibus.
15	Winter creeps	6 6.6 6.	Suo-gân.

PRINTED IN GREAT BRITAIN AT THE UNIVERSITY PRESS, OXFORD
BY JOHN JOHNSON, PRINTER TO THE UNIVERSITY

1 ⎫
2 ⎬ morn.   87
3° ⎬   90
5° ⎭   91° general
9° Eve.   93° ⎤
14 Sun   98°
17 ⎫   100
19° ⎬ Christmas 103° ✓
20° ⎬   106
23 ⎭
33 angels   107°
36 ⎤   111
38°
39 general   Total 48. (younger children° 25)
42°
43°
46 (world?)
49°
50°
51°
53°
56 (June)
58°
60°
64
67
69°
70
72°
73
77°
78
79°
81°
82
83
84
85°